Web geek's Guide

to

Google™ Chrome

WITHDRAWN

Jerri Ledford
Yvette Davis

800 East 96th Street,
Indianapolis, Indiana 46240

Web Geek's Guide to Google Chrome

ISBN-13: 978-0-7897-3973-5
ISBN-10: 0-7897-3973-9

Library of Congress Cataloging-in-Publication Data:

Ledford, Jerri L.
  Web geek's guide to Google Chrome / Jerri Ledford, Yvette Davis. —
1st ed.
      p. cm.
  Includes index.
  ISBN 978-0-7897-3973-5
  1. Browsers (Computer programs) 2. Google chrome. I. Davis, Yvette.
II. Title.
  TK5105.883.G66L43 2009
  025.04252—dc22

                                        2009014447

Printed in the United States of America

Second Printing June 2009

Trademarks

All terms mentioned in this book that are known to be trademarks or service marks have been appropriately capitalized. Que Publishing cannot attest to the accuracy of this information. Use of a term in this book should not be regarded as affecting the validity of any trademark or service mark.

Warning and Disclaimer

Every effort has been made to make this book as complete and as accurate as possible, but no warranty or fitness is implied. The information provided is on an "as is" basis. The authors and the publisher shall have neither liability nor responsibility to any person or entity with respect to any loss or damages arising from the information contained in this book.

Bulk Sales

Que Publishing offers excellent discounts on this book when ordered in quantity for bulk purchases or special sales. For more information, please contact

> **U.S. Corporate and Government Sales**
> **1-800-382-3419**
> **corpsales@pearsontechgroup.com**

For sales outside of the U.S., please contact

> **International Sales**
> **international@pearson.com**

Associate Publisher
Greg Wiegand

Acquisitions Editor
Michelle Newcomb

Development Editor
Todd Brakke

Managing Editor
Kristy Hart

Senior Project Editor
Matthew Purcell

Copy Editor
Geneil Breeze

Indexer
Cheryl Lenser

Proofreader
Kathy Ruiz

Technical Editor
Vince Averello

Publishing Coordinator
Cindy Teeters

Book Designer
Anne Jones

Compositor
Nonie Ratcliff

Contents at a Glance

Table of Contents

Part II: Tinkering Around Under the Hood

About the Author

Jerri Ledford has been a freelance business technology writer for more than 10 years. During that time, more than 1,000 of her articles, profiles, news stories, and reports have appeared online and in print. Her publishing credits include *Intelligent Enterprise*, *Network World*, *Information Security Magazine*, *DCM magazine*, *CRM magazine*, *IT Manager's Journal*, and dozens more.

Jerri also develops and teaches technology training courses for both consumer and business users. Some of the course topics she's been involved with include security, customer service, career skills, and technology for companies such as IBT Financial, Writer's Village University, Beacon Hill Financial Services, Hewlett-Packard, Sony, and CNET.

She is the author of 17 books including *Google Analytics*, *Google Powered: Productivity with Online Tools*, *Google Analytics 2.0*, *The Search Engine Optimization Bible*, *Google AdSense for Dummies*, *The Search Engine Optimization Bible, Second Edition*, and *The Web Geek's Guide to the Android-Enabled Phone*.

In her time off Jerri travels extensively and enjoys hiking, writing fiction novels, and soaking up the positive ions at the beach with her children.

Yvette Davis writes on a variety of topics, but her passions are all things open source and alternative medicine. Yvette is the managing editor for the Google Channel on Brighthub.com, and she is a contributing editor for the Linux Channel on the same site. She also writes alternative health articles.

Dedication

From Jerri Ledford:

For my children, because of all the people in the world, you always believe in me. Thanks, guys. I love you.
—Mom

From Yvette Davis:

For Crystal, Nicole, Justin, AJ, Jen, Bryanna, and Allan. Without you, it wouldn't have been possible.

For Kathryn, for always believing.

For Mrs. B, for insisting dreams could be lived.

Acknowledgments

It takes so many people to put a book together, and not all of the names end up on the cover. Fortunately, some do, and I owe a hardy thank you to my coauthor, Yvette Davis. Yvette is not only brilliant, but I swear there must be three of her. This woman handles a workload like none I've ever seen. Without her, the book would be only half of what it is. Thank you, Ma'am.

Derek Torres, also was instrumental in the pages that you see here. Derek, you were a lifesaver. I hope to one day return the favor.

Of course, there are also all those people behind the scenes whose names I don't know more often than not. Lynn Haller is one of those whose names I do know, and she deserves far more than simple kudos. Lynn, your hard work and persistence have paid off, again! Thank you so much.

The team at Que is also to be commended. Michelle Newcomb and Todd Brakke are the names I know; there are probably a dozen or so more whose names I don't know. I thank all of you for your efforts. My part in this book was easy. Yours helps make the book successful.

Finally, thanks to the readers, as always, for picking up the book. I hope you find everything that you're looking for in these pages. —Jerri Ledford

My deepest thanks and appreciation to Jerri and Lynn for bringing me in on this project. —Yvette Davis

We Want to Hear from You!

As the reader of this book, *you* are our most important critic and commentator. We value your opinion and want to know what we're doing right, what we could do better, what areas you'd like to see us publish in, and any other words of wisdom you're willing to pass our way.

As an associate publisher for Que Publishing, I welcome your comments. You can email or write me directly to let me know what you did or didn't like about this book—as well as what we can do to make our books better.

Please note that I cannot help you with technical problems related to the topic of this book. We do have a User Services group, however, where I will forward specific technical questions related to the book.

When you write, please be sure to include this book's title and author as well as your name, email address, and phone number. I will carefully review your comments and share them with the author and editors who worked on the book.

Email: feedback@quepublishing.com

Mail: Greg Wiegand
           Associate Publisher
           Que Publishing
           800 East 96th Street
           Indianapolis, IN 46240 USA

Reader Services

Visit our website and register this book at informit.com/register for convenient access to any updates, downloads, or errata that might be available for this book.

Introduction

Seems that everything is web-based these days. From paying your bills, to making restaurant reservations, and even watching television, there just isn't much that you can't do using the Web. And we're raising a whole generation of people who can't imagine living without the Web.

There was a time, and many of you probably remember it, when we didn't have a Web—at least, not like it is now. There was an Internet that scholars used to exchange ideas and information, but in the bigger picture, the Internet that we know today is much, much improved from its humble beginnings.

Imagine how it's going to change over the course of the next decade or two. If the Internet already invades every aspect of our daily lives, by the time our kids have kids, it will be a requirement of daily living. And that's where browsers like Google Chrome come into the picture.

Chrome is designed to help you use the Web in ways that work for you. It's the first step toward an Internet that's different from what we know now. But it's not so advanced that we can't use it right now.

Chrome Changes Surfing

One of the coolest things about Google Chrome is that it's different from any other web browser that you've ever used—just not so different that it's difficult or uncomfortable to use. Sure, some features and changes take some time getting used to (and you learn about those in this book), but you can install Chrome and begin using it pretty efficiently almost immediately.

What Chrome does, however, is change the way you surf. If you can get used to the minimalist design of the browser, you quickly find that it's far more user friendly than other browsers that are available. It's also much more powerful.

Everything is handled differently in Chrome with one goal in mind: to make surfing (and interacting with) the Web a faster, more efficient part of our daily lives. That means the browser handles web pages better and faster. And it gives you just enough control to allow you to truly interact with the Web in a give-and-take fashion.

Of course, before you can fully take advantage of all that Chrome has to offer, you have to understand all the details about the concept of Chrome and about how to use it. That's what this book brings to the table. In the following chapters, you find everything you need to use Chrome—even to make it completely your own.

How It's Put Together

We tried to put the book together in a manner that makes sense to you. Of course, we covered everything from the most basic use of Chrome to more advanced, really get your hands into the innards, features. And we tried to cover it so that no matter who you are, you get something from every page of the book.

Part I: Google Chrome and Browsing the Way It Should Be

The book is broken into three parts. Each part is designed to move you from basic to more advanced use of Google Chrome. If you're already using Chrome, some of the information in the beginning of the book might only require a quick perusal. We do encourage you to at least skim through even the basic chapters, though, because you learn concepts like

- **Chapter 1, "Web Interactions Past and Present"**—If you want to know why Google would enter the Browser Wars, this chapter gives you some insight. Of course, the actual facts surrounding Google's decision to build and release Chrome are something Google will never actually share with anyone, but the information in this chapter makes some intuitive leaps of understanding based on educated guesses.

- **Chapter 2, "What Google Chrome Brings to the Browser"**—In this chapter, you learn how Chrome is different from other browsers. There's even a comparison to some of the other browsers that you might be more familiar with.

- **Chapter 3, "Getting Started with Google Chrome"**—The first time that you use Google Chrome, it's going to seem very strange. This chapter walks you through installing Chrome and helps you to prepare for what you (won't) see the first time you take it for a spin.

- **Chapter 4, "It's Everything: The Omnibox (Plus Some)"**—One of the key differences of Chrome, from a user's perspective is the Omnibox. You might think of it as the address bar. There's much more to it than just addresses, though. And while we're sharing the "much more" part, this chapter gives you a closer look at other facets of Chrome that offer additional features.

- **Chapter 5, "Stability on the Net"**—Ever had a web browser crash while you were in the middle of something? If you have, you know how frustrating it can be. This chapter helps you to understand how Chrome can protect you from the angst of a browser crash.

- **Chapter 6, "Safe Browsing on a Threatening Web"**—These days, you find security threats at every turn on the Internet. Chrome is designed to help keep you safe from many of those threats, and this chapter explains those safety features to you in detail.

Part II: Tinkering Around Under the Hood

If you're a tinkerer, this part of the book is really for you. In the chapters in Part II, we really get into what makes Chrome work—and what you can do with it.

Chrome is based on open source software, which means that large parts of it are available for you to tweak until your heart's content. What exactly do you need to know to start making Chrome your own? Here's the list:

- **Chapter 7, "An Open Source Overview"**—This chapter walks you through exactly what open source is and how it affects what you can do with Chrome. You also find out what some of the components of Chrome that you'll have access to are.

- **Chapter 8, "Developing Sites for Chrome"**—If you have a website, you probably don't want to leave Google Chrome users out of those who can view it. But there are a few things that you need to understand before you begin to develop websites for Google Chrome. This chapter is where you learn all about those.

- **Chapter 9, "Spit-Shining Chrome"**—If you've done any Internet research about Chrome at all, you know it's a minimalistic browser—at least in appearance. However, that doesn't mean you can't tweak its appearance to make it more visually appealing to you. You can. And in this chapter, you learn how.

- **Chapter 10, "Make It Yours"**—The last chapter in this part is all about making Chrome feel like a browser that was created especially for you. In this chapter you learn some of the customization tricks that help you to take full advantage of all that Chrome has to offer.

Part III: Chrome for Power Users

This is the shortest part of the book, but it's probably got some of the most exciting information about Chrome in it. In just two chapters, this part shows you all the capabilities that you want if you're a power user and how to fix the problems that you might face along the way.

Chapter 11, "Chrome Hacks for the Power User," is where you're going to find a few little tricks that just blow your mind. By the time you get to Chapter 11, you've already looked at more simplistic capabilities earlier in the book, but you better roll up your sleeves for these, because they're all just one step more.

And of course, no matter how well a piece of software is designed, you're going to face the occasional problem. That's what **Chapter 12, "Troubleshooting Google Chrome,"** is for. In this chapter, we walk you through some of the most frequently encountered problems and how to fix them.

The Appendices

Appendix A, "Google Chrome Shortcuts," you might find handy, as it lists all the keyboard shortcuts that you can use with Chrome. You're already familiar with some of the shortcuts; others are probably new to you.

There are several pages of shortcuts to take advantage of. And if you do happen to come across something that you haven't seen before, make note of it. Highlight it. Or even post it on a note next to your computer so that you can begin using it. These shortcuts help you reduce the time it takes to perform common tasks in Chrome.

Appendix B, "Chrome for the Non-Window User"—gives you an overview of CrossOver Chromium for those using a Linux or Macintosh operating system.

Finally, Appendix C is a glossary of key terms we have talked about in the book.

Special Features

As you're reading through the chapters, you'll come across a set of special features designed to help you pull out important bits of information about the subjects being covered. Those features include

 Geek Speak—Jargon is frustrating. We do our best to avoid jargon whenever possible, but sometimes it's not possible. So, you find jargon words defined in clear language in these pullouts.

 No Joke—Careful! You could damage your device or lose data in some places. There are also other issues that you might need a warning about. These are not joking matters, so this box provides the cautions that you need to avoid damaging the device, application, or data as you work through the steps in the book.

Yellow Box—In the Google culture, the Yellow Box is a search appliance that leads to additional information. Our Yellow Box performs the same function. If there's more that you might need to know—a tip or trick that's useful or even just a few sentences of deeper information that clarifies a concept for you—you find it in the Yellow Box.

Privileged Information—Sometimes there's really interesting information related to the topic at hand, but it's not completely relevant to the steps we're walking you through or the information that we're giving you. Maybe it's just something that additional information might make it easier for you to understand and use. In those cases, a sidebar provides the privileged information you need or at least a pointer to get you headed in the right direction.

Each of these features contains information that helps make this book more useful to you. So, keep your eyes open for the special elements. They're your clue that more information is available that you might find useful.

Who Should Read This Book?

If you've picked up the book and gotten this far into the introduction, it's a good bet that you're part of the audience for the book. We're writing to those who are both beginners and intermediate users. Beginners will find all the information that they need to get started using Google Chrome, whereas intermediate users will find additional tips and tricks that they might not have known about as well as information on programming Chrome widgets and features.

Now, to be honest, if you're an advanced user, you'll probably only find review information in these pages, but the occasional review is good. Often, as we advance into the upper levels of the user kingdom, we forget or overlook some of the basic and simple uses, practices, and applications. So, even advanced users might benefit from a quick skimming of the pages that you find here.

Above all, our goal is to help readers use Google Chrome to the fullest extent possible. We want you to be as excited about Chrome as we are, so we worked hard to pass on all the information that we can to help you make the most of Google Chrome.

Of course, things change. And by the time this book hits the shelves, there will have been many changes that we were not able to cover. So, we set up a website to help you track those changes. The website, http://www.WebGeeksGuide. com, contains a blog where regular updates about Chrome as well as other Google applications will appear. You may also find additional training materials when they're available for new features and applications. And of course, we welcome your comments about this or any of the other Web Geek's Guides on the website. Use the **Contact Us** link as often as you want.

Okay, we've blabbered on long enough about the basics and features of the book. Now, we'll let you get on with reading the book. We hope you find the information that you seek and it's presented in a way that makes it easy for you to use. Thanks for reading!

Google Chrome and Browsing the Way It Should Be

In this part:

- Web Interactions Past and Present
- What Google Chrome Brings to the Browser
- Getting Started with Google Chrome
- It's Everything: The Omnibox (Plus Some)
- Stability on the Net
- Safe Browsing on a Threatening Web

Google Chrome jumped into the Browser Wars well after the fight had started, and people around the world wondered, "Why?" After all, some great web browsers are already available, what could Google possibly bring to the table that was any different?

Hold on to your hats, because the answer is: so much! This part of the book introduces you to a possible mind-set behind Chrome as well as actually walks you through some of the differences that Chrome brings to the Browser Wars. For a latecomer, it's pretty well prepared for battle.

Of course, along the way you learn some basics about how to use Chrome. And as always, the chapters (with the exception of Chapter 1, which is mostly explanation) are visual. Many screen shots help you stay on track as you work through all the information.

So, let's get started. There's a lot of ground to cover.

Web Interactions Past and Present

The day that Chrome was released for public use, the Internet was afire with theories and conjecture about what Google's ultimate goal behind the release is.

It was brave, after all, for Google to enter the Browser Wars this late in the game. It's like coming to a tennis tournament and taking on the top rated players in the last two brackets of the tournament. If you're an unknown player, no one is going to know what to expect.

And no one knew what to expect from Google's Chrome, either. Is Google trying to take over the Web? Or maybe it's creating a web-based operating system? What in the world is going on?

Of course, we have no idea what the people at Google were thinking when they created Chrome, or what the plans are now that Chrome is available, but we can look at the environment and make a few solid guesses.

The Theory of the Web-Based Operating System

The best place to start with our educated guessing is probably the Web. Since Google is known for its web-based applications, and since one of the first cries heard 'round the world when Chrome was released was "Google's creating a web-based operating system," let's look at the Web and how it's used today.

For starters, web capabilities are better than they've ever been. Broadband users are the norm now, not the exception. And it seems like every company on the planet not only has a website but some web-based functionality, too. We're an Internet society, there's no denying that.

That said, however, the debate is where we stand as an Internet society. Currently, we have computers that we use to do almost everything, including accessing the Internet and all the tasks that we perform on the Internet. But a particular group of people would prefer that we use the computer only for accessing the Web and put everything that we do on the Web—a true Internet society.

A *Star Trek*-esque Society

In a world like that, the Web would be your operating system, and your applications would all be accessible from that point. Think *Star Trek* or some of the other Sci-Fi shows that you might have seen (*Aeon Flux* comes to mind) where everything is accessible from a single interface—like our browser. That's a web-based operating system.

What's so cool about a web-based operating system that it would be the goal that we think every technology company is striving to achieve? Well, for starters, Internet-based applications would allow for much better resource sharing between applications. Every application could be tied into every other application, so there would be no need to perform a task one time over here, then another time over there, and yet another somewhere else.

You could perform that task one time, it would automatically be replicated in all the other places that the information is needed, and the next time you access an application that needs that data, it's available. Your only input is that single point of entry.

Web-Based OS Is for the Future

Moving back to current times, capabilities for a web-based operating system (and by extension a web-based society) don't yet exist. For starters, we're far too dependent on our current hard-drive based software applications. Add to that the fact that we're also far too paranoid about personal security and privacy (as we should be in *most* cases), and there are still so many problems to overcome with a web-based operating system that it's still a decade or so down the road.

The truth is, it's likely to be about the time our kids are having kids before a true web-based operating system starts to take hold. About that time, kids will have been completely immersed in the web-based world that we now live in. Right now, there are still a lot of us who remember a world without the Internet.

Okay, we hear you screaming, "This is all very interesting, but what does it have to do with Google Chrome?" Simply this: When Chrome was released, many people believed that it was a major coup in Google's quest for a web-based operating system, even though it's still too early for that kind of OS to take hold. This is not to say that Google wasn't completely on the money with the idea that a web browser based on open source programming was the right move. It's just that other factors come into play here.

See, Google Chrome is not a web-based operating system in disguise. Google Chrome is a web browser based on an open source software platform that Google is using to prepare for the future.

Here's where it gets interesting. Part of the intrigue about Google Chrome is that it's built on a platform that's similar to Google's mobile operating system—Android. And it's my belief that Google is working on a way to merge the two, which of course, is the first step to creating a web-based operating system.

Mobility Must Come First

Before there can be a web-based operating system, there must be a way to access that operating system that works seamlessly with our lives. In all those Sci-Fi flicks that you watch, you don't see people stopping everything to run to their computer to find the information that they need.

No! They pull a device *out of their pocket* that they use to access the information...information that, incidentally, is delivered to them over the mobile web. Now we're getting somewhere. A key component of the web-based operating system will be the ability to access it on-the-fly, from multiple devices that are about the size of a deck of cards (or smaller). We're not there yet.

That doesn't meant that Google can't begin preparing for the time when that's a capability, though. And, yes, Google will likely be at the forefront of that movement.

Openness Is the Key to Mobility Is the Key to...

Openness has already started with the creation of the *Open Handset Alliance*—a group of future-minded companies that realize that the future of technology is in the palm of your hand. People have always lusted after technology in the smallest form factor with the most functionality. Had we not, computers would still take up entire rooms in our homes.

The *Open Handset Alliance* is a group of mobile technology companies, that have come together to work on creating an "open" mobile web. Currently, mobility is ruled by proprietary technologies. You're either with one company or you're with another. The goal of the Open Handset Alliance is to create mobility without borders or walls where mobile devices and mobile applications all work together to achieve a single goal—providing users with the service and applications that they want and need.

Don't misunderstand. Many companies are striving to reach the mobility level that people demand. The problem is that most of those companies don't realize that their own proprietary platforms will eventually make them obsolete. Proprietary software and applications, by their very nature will exclude those companies from advancement, because what users want is openness.

Twice now, I've referred to Sci-Fi films. There's a reason for that. The people who create the stories that those films are based on are people just like you and me. What's more, they have the same wants and needs that you and I have: the ability to decrease the stresses of life as much as possible using the technologies at hand.

And the technologies that you see in those Sci-Fi films are often prototypes. Some of them will never become devices or technologies that are available to us. Some will take on very different formats before they're finally available to us, and some will eventually become exactly as we saw them a decade earlier in a really cool movie about the future.

The way that those technologies come about, however, is through collaboration. Yes, an author might think up something that sounds cool. But chances are, she's going to go looking for a real technology that's similar to what she's looking for. If the technology creators kept those "fictional" technologies completely to themselves, without sharing their capabilities with others, they would never see the light of day—they would never be anything more than proprietary technology.

For technology to advance to what it will eventually be, there has to be a sharing of ideas. One genius has to say to another, "That's great, but what if it did this, too?" And that's where Google is one step ahead of everyone else. (You thought I was never going to get back around to Chrome, didn't you?)

Google's release of the Google Chrome web browser is revolutionary in two different ways. First, there's the fact that it is a web browser with many ties to the mobile world. But the other facet of Chrome that many other technology companies seem to be missing is that, with the release of Chrome, Google can do something that it's famous for—something that has helped Google to move from just a search engine company to a real technological contender.

It allows Google to study how people use the Internet.

Browsing in an Application-Driven World

I bet a shiver ran down your spine when you read the last sentence of the preceding section. If not, you're probably a true geek like me. I don't have a problem in the world with Google studying how I use the Internet—as long as they do it without violating some basic privacy tenants.

However, that's not the stance that most folks take when they think of Google. More often than not, conspiracy theory fear takes over, and people believe that Google is tracking our movements to use against us. I haven't yet heard of a single person exploited by the information that Google collects.

What's missing in the Google-tracking equation is understanding. Many people don't understand that what Google is tracking isn't personal information, it's movements on the Web. And they aren't tracking a person, so much as they're tracking an unidentifiable number.

They're looking for patterns, not information that can be used to exploit you in any way.

Chaos, Fallen Orderly

What makes Google, Google, is that it analyzes data and finds patterns. Think about this. Millions of people each day surf the Web. To follow each of those people and to keep a detailed record of all their movements would be so resource intensive that it might as well be impossible.

But, if you could follow key patterns in those movements, you might be on to something. And that's what Google is good at. In addition to finding those patterns, though, Google also analyzes them to find out what people want online.

They've found that people want to accomplish something. The Internet that used to be strictly for entertainment is no longer just a diversion. It's become a tool that people use to get through their daily lives. Productivity, communication, *and* entertainment are all part of that.

To take advantage of that, Google, like many other companies, has started to build web-based applications. These applications are available from anywhere there is an Internet connection, making them far more useful than their computer-based brothers. (Are you starting to see a pattern here?)

People are adopting web-based applications at an impressive rate. The growth in web-based office applications is astounding. So, much so, in fact, that even Microsoft is getting into the act with its suite of Windows Live applications.

Web-Based from the Ground Up

The problem with applications like those Microsoft offers being web-based at this point is that they were originally computer-based programs. In most cases, they're clinging to the original limiting parameters used to create the applications.

Google applications, on the other hand, were built from the ground up to be web-based. That means they're built to take advantage of spaces without walls and limitations that would prevent certain features. Adding the Google Chrome browser to that mix only makes sense.

Think of it this way. We live in houses. And we decorate and use our houses according to the amount of space that we have. Now, what if you didn't live in a house. What if you lived in a wide open space with no limitations or boundaries? How much more could you do with that space? What would you add? What new ways would you interact with the space?

That's how Google's web-based applications are. They're not subject to the same limitations as are other applications. And adding Google Chrome to the mix just adds functionality. The browsers available before Chrome were designed to fit the Web to our existing world.

All too often, that meant not enough power or resources to do what we wanted to do with the applications that we did find online. Or, perhaps we could access and use those applications, but we had to do it according to the parameters set forth by the browser. Chrome changes that because it's a browser designed to work *with* those web-based applications.

A good example of how this works is the way that Chrome handles links. In previous browsers, you had to open a link according to the parameters of the browser in which you were interacting with said link. You could right click it and choose from a menu of options (sometimes) such as opening it in a new window or a new tab. But with Chrome, opening a link in a new tab is as simply as a click and drag movement—you click the link you want to open and drag it to the tab bar to open the link in a new tab. You can also interact with the right click window to open the link in another window or even a 'private' window that's not traceable. In other words, you can interact with links in the manner that works best for you.

Ultimately, Chrome is designed to be the browser that allows you the freedom to interact with the Web, rather than to simply use the Web. It has the power, speed, and security to allow you to use web-based applications in the manner that they're meant to be used (with Google's apps being right there at the forefront, of course).

Closing the Door

So, to answer the questions raised at the beginning of this chapter: "Is Google trying to take over the Web?" and "Is Google creating a web-based operating system?" The answer in both cases is yes...and no.

Google is taking advantage of the technology that is available, monitoring how people use that technology, and improving on it with a clear picture of what the future will most likely look like. But it's not doing it maliciously.

Chrome is a good example of how Google is using what it's learning about people and how they interact with the Web. It's a fully functional, completely usable browser with the potential to be the best tool you've ever used.

Of course, before it can become that, you need to know how to use it. And now that I'm finished explaining my take on what Google's intent for Chrome is, it's time to learn just that. Chapter 2, "What Google Chrome Brings to the Browser," starts your education with an explanation of what Chrome has to offer. Here's a hint: It could be what helps them, the latecomers, win the Browser Wars.

What Google Chrome Brings to the Browser

You finally decided to break free of the chains that bind you. After years of putting up with the Pepsi versus Coke battle of web browsers, you finally decided to get past it and look elsewhere. Congratulations!

Many people haven't decided to take the leap, but Chrome is prepared to reward you for your choice. If you did any research on Chrome prior to downloading it, there's a good chance that you know most of what's in this chapter. If you didn't, or if you aren't familiar with Chrome, then sit back, relax, and enjoy a leisurely read of Chapter 2. In this chapter you learn a few things about how Chrome is different from any other browser you've used in the past.

2

NOT Your Momma's Web Browser

When you open up Chrome, it's kind of hard to miss the obvious—web browsers sure have come a long way over the years! While most of our "mommas" (so to speak) probably didn't enjoy web browsers until well after we did, it's unbelievable how far Internet technology has come since the days of Mosaic way back in 1993! It seems like yesterday to some of us, but in Internet time, that's an eternity.

Back in those very early days of web browsing, we didn't really care about modern day bogeymen such as spyware, pop-up ads, phishing, and so on. At that time, the web browser was a means to check out our first website with the black text on a funky purple background that was impossible to read (Hello world!) or to check out some really badly designed corporate websites that most companies today would prefer you not remember. The Internet has come a long way since then.

Chrome ushers us into a new era, where web surfing isn't as innocent and safe as we hoped it might always be. It puts security and peace of mind at the forefront of its features, yet in a way that even nontechie types can create and enjoy a safe surfing environment without stressing out about it.

More than that, Chrome is not just a casual surfer's web browser; it also has developers in mind. Not content with being a conduit to downloading music and reading the news, it also remembers those who make technology what it is today—the computer programmers. Chrome has a special place reserved for you, so that you can view your code or debug your JavaScript, for example.

Let's not lose sight of that fact that Chrome is still in its infancy as a web browser; in fact, its current official release is still in the 2.x family. Unfortunately, Chrome suffers from the "child star" syndrome.

It was forced to "grow up" in the shadow of a famous parent (Google) and in an industry of big stars (Internet Explorer, Safari, Opera, and Firefox—just to name a few). So, there was a lot of pressure for Chrome to perform well right out of the gate. With an impressive start already under the belt, Chrome is sure to continually improve and include some of the more glaring omissions in the near future.

Chrome is also revolutionary in ways that aren't readily apparent. The good folks at Google decided to create a web browser destined to be a leader, not a follower. That's why it includes a powerful *JavaScript engine*—which translates code into actions faster than any other method currently available—and other performance optimizations that set this browser several light years ahead of what you and your momma used back in the early 1990s.

geek speak

A *JavaScript engine* is basically an interpreter for your computer. It interprets JavaScript source code into actions. In other words, it decodes a script (that is seemingly in a foreign language) and executes the actions coded into that script.

Even though Chrome is definitely not your momma's web browser of yore, it certainly is one that she is going to love using. But how does Chrome stand up compared to the other titans of web browsing?

Comparing Chrome to Other Browsers

Although Chrome has the advantage of having a high-tech heavyweight behind it, that doesn't necessarily mean it's going to be a hit, or even worth using. Over the years, we've seen a number of "good ideas" fall by the wayside, such as Mosaic, NetCaptor, and Netscape. So, how does Chrome size up? Let's take a look at how it fares against some of the current industry standards: Internet Explorer, Firefox, and Opera.

Internet Explorer

Internet Explorer definitely has its place in the pantheon of web browsers; since it first hit the Web in 1995, it quickly became a leading web browser and evolved into the browser to beat. Since beating Microsoft is a challenge for almost any software editor, it certainly drew its fare share of competitors.

As I write this, Internet Explorer 7, shown in Figure 2.1, is the official version available; however, by the time you read this text Microsoft will have released Internet Explorer 8 into the wild. So, we use that as our basis of comparison in this section. After all, IE 8 is clearly meant to defend its position against the young upstart.

One of Chrome's biggest advantages is that it doesn't carry all the baggage that Microsoft's Internet Explorer does—literally and figuratively! Internet Explorer evokes strong feelings upon mere mention of its name; whether you love it or hate it, very few web users are ever indifferent to Internet Explorer.

On a literal level, Chrome is minimalist in its approach. Comparatively, Internet Explorer follows a more everything-but-the-kitchen-sink approach to *user interface*.

FIGURE 2.1

Internet Explorer 7 is different from Chrome in both appearance and performance.

geek speak   *User interface* is simply the part of the application that users see and interact with. In terms of our browser comparison, Chrome has few buttons and tools integrated into the part of the browser that you see. On the other hand, Internet Explorer has tons of buttons and tools built right into the top of the browser. For some this is handy; for others, it's clutter.

From a pure user perspective, it seems as if Internet Explorer wants to dazzle you with its bells and whistles. Chrome, by comparison, offers many of the same bells and whistles but emphasizes the website itself instead of the actual web browser. That, after all, is why you opened a web browser in the first place.

This is evidenced in the download differences of the two programs. Internet Explorer is a time-consuming download and installation process. It can take over an hour to be ready to use IE, even when you're using broadband for the download. Google's Chrome, however, is a nearly instantaneous download and installation. It literally takes just minutes to have it installed and ready to use.

From experience, Chrome also loads considerably faster out of the gate. In fact, Chrome launches virtually immediately and is fully operational almost as fast. In literally no time at all, Chrome is ready to roll and offers you both bookmarks and thumbnail views of recently visited sites, as shown in Figure 2.2.

Recent bookmarks

Bookmark bar

Additional bookmarks

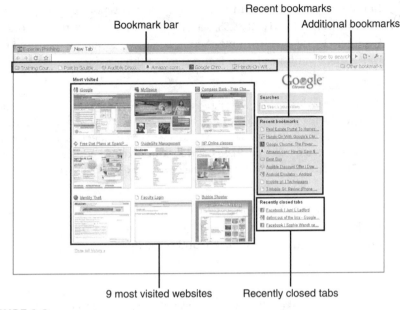

9 most visited websites   Recently closed tabs

FIGURE 2.2

Chrome is ready to serve—offering both bookmarks and recently visited sites.

Internet Explorer, on the other hand, takes the scenic route as it loads. Of course, you must consider two important pieces of information: We're not working with a final release of Internet Explorer, and Internet Explorer simply has so much to load!

Internet Explorer goes well beyond the requirements of a simple web browser and really tries to integrate into your whole home computer experience. For example, Internet Explorer 8 can integrate with Microsoft Office's OneNote or Windows Live Writer for blogging. For whatever reason, Microsoft believes that it's always good to have a finger in every pie. And while it might be good in theory, in practice adding all that stuff to the browser really slows it down and reduces the effectiveness of the core functionality—browsing the Web.

While it may seem contradictory, Internet Explorer isn't good at sharing applications, even though Microsoft wants you to have access to a ton of different applications. So, what happens is that the browser gets bloated with a ton of overlap information. That overlap drains resources and gums up the works. Chrome, on the other hand, shares resources where it can, which streamlines the mechanism, making everything work faster and more efficiently.

Internet Explorer, however, is superior when it comes to developer tools. To be fair, Chrome offers some basic developer tools, but this is one area where

Internet Explorer shines. In fact, it even offers a separate *developer browser* that lets you work with HTML, CSS, scripts, and so on. In this respect, Internet Explorer clearly bests Chrome. Again, these are developer tools and casual web surfers won't need such features to get the job done.

> **geek speak** A *developer browser* is a browser designed for use by developers. Often, that means a separate toolbar that attaches to your browser that allows you to validate code and view web pages as if you were in a development environment. To activate Chrome's developer features, click the **Page Controls** icon, and then navigate to and hover over **Developer**. Then you can select the developer options that you need.

Chrome may not have the experience or add-on rich interface that Internet Explorer provides, but it is a solid competitor if you want a no-frills web browser that loads pages quickly and correctly.

Firefox

Firefox is most likely the biggest competitor or threat to Internet Explorer at the moment. In addition to being an efficient web browser, it also has legions of fans—including both those who like the browser on its merits and those who have a visceral dislike for anything Microsoft. Chrome, by comparison, is more of a second cousin to Firefox than it is to Internet Explorer.

First, both Chrome and Firefox enjoy a relatively simple user interface. The bells and whistles that Internet Explorer proudly displays are more discreetly available in Chrome and Firefox. However, there are some *out-of-the-box* differences, as shown in Figure 2.3.

> **geek speak** *Out-of-the-box* is a term you've probably heard in reference to software a lot. It means that you can use the software without any customization at all; you simply download it, install it, and then start using it. Of course, customization might still be possible—tweaking it to your preferences—but it's not required to accomplish the core function of software. In other words, you can use it straight out of the box.

Chrome once again launches considerably faster than Firefox. Of course, this is somewhat anecdotal and may differ depending on your hardware. However, in writing this book, the difference was visually evident. Once Firefox is open, it springs to life and quickly displays the default home page.

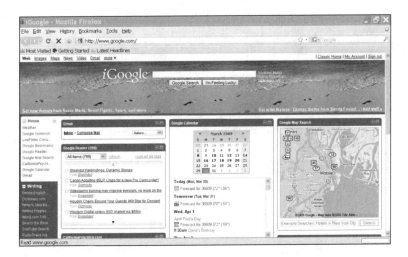

FIGURE 2.3

Firefox and Chrome are somewhat similar in appearance, though Chrome is even more basic than Firefox.

Like Chrome, Firefox is a relatively simple user interface that provides just the minimum of shortcuts and buttons on the toolbar. Unlike Chrome, Firefox offers an impressive array of *extensions* to soup up your web browser.

geek speak

Extensions are bits of functionality that extend the usability of the browser. For example, a Firefox extension called FireFTP is an FTP application that works within your browser to allow you to access and interact with FTP sites.

In Chrome each tab is an individual process. This is a huge advantage over Firefox when surfing multiple sites within a single window, as shown in Figure 2.4.

What that means for you in non-geek talk is that if you are using Chrome and have three different websites open in three different tabs and one of the websites stops responding, only that tab crashes. This gives Chrome the distinct advantage of letting you simply isolate a "rogue" tab and shut it down rather than losing the content of your other tabs by having to shut down and restart the entire web browser.

Of course, Firefox is now a well-developed web browser that has had time to grow and learn from its earlier mistakes. Even though Firefox is still an all-around more solid web browser, Chrome definitely offers a viable alternative for those who want to get away from the two dominant players in the Browser Wars.

Individual tabs

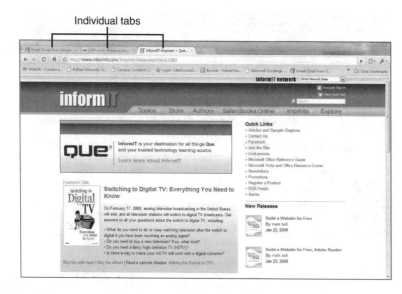

FIGURE 2.4

Tabs are a common feature these days, but Chrome lets you localize a crash down to a single tab so your entire browser doesn't crash.

Opera

Opera is the third and final browser to take the Chrome challenge. If Chrome is a distant cousin of Firefox, then Opera (shown in Figure 2.5) is like the refined, cultured cousin that doesn't want to admit it's related to Internet Explorer.

While Chrome adopts the minimalist approach to a point of perfection of which even Samuel Beckett would be proud, Opera eschews this theory and goes for the "more is more" approach—and manages to pull it off. At the end of the day, both web browsers offer a solid product, where Chrome is better in some respects and Opera is better in others. The choice is ultimately down to what is more important to you—performance or features.

When it comes to features, Chrome is usually markedly superior to Opera. The reason that statement is qualified by "usually" is because different *benchmarking* tests take into consideration different factors. More often than not, Chrome bested Opera in speed and performance during these trials.

FIGURE 2.5
Opera looks a lot like Chrome, only it offers more features but less performance.

geek speak

Benchmarking is a frequently used term in computer jargon for submitting an application (Chrome in this case) for rigorous performance testing using industry standard tests to measure performance. These results allow technologists and consumers to compare hardware and software objectively.

Earlier in the chapter, we mentioned that Chrome doesn't offer all the *add-ins* that Internet Explorer and Firefox both do. This is also the case compared to Opera, which offers *widgets* (similar to Microsoft *gadgets*) to help improve usability, or at least facilitate it. Chrome does, however, offer features typical of most decent web browsers. Opera also offers a robust, complete user interface that is a 180-degree turn from Chrome's basic aesthetic. Where Opera succeeds is that it manages to do this without coming across as cluttered.

geek speak

Add-ins, *widgets*, and *gadgets* are essentially the same as extensions. They're bits of applications, or mini-applications, that offer additional functionality that operates with an application. You see widgets and gadgets used more often in reference to sidebar applications and add-ins, and extensions are usually used to reference browsers and other applications, such as Microsoft Word.

Again, it comes down to what you expect and what you ultimately need from your web browser. Chrome offers you a complete web surfing experience, in that it handles graphics and multimedia without trouble. Opera offers a full-bodied experience, but one that can be slightly slower than what you experience with Chrome. Like any product or brand, your ultimate choice likely comes down to your personal preferences.

Speed Depends on How You Handle the Code

Mankind has always been fascinated by speed—be it cars, airplanes, or web browsers. When it comes to speed and web browsers, it's important to differentiate web browser performance (based on its inner workings) and network performance. Even the fastest web browser in the world will not make a big difference you if you are using a dial-up Internet connection.

Most benchmark tests currently available show Chrome to be one of the fastest, if not the fastest, web browsers on the market. Google's own benchmarks show a curiously positive result, which makes it somewhat dubious. However, a number of other tests are available online that demonstrate performance that is nothing short of impressive.

What is Chrome's secret? After all, Chrome is using *Java Virtual Machine (JVM)*, which is hardly revolutionary, right? Wrong! Google created a souped-up version of JVM for use with Chrome called the *V8 JavaScript Engine*. If you're into cars, or simply even own a car, you can appreciate the message that Google is sending with the V8 moniker.

---

geek speak The *Java Virtual Machine (JVM)* is a set of programs that run Java programs in a virtual environment. This frees resources for other applications, which prevents your system from slowing down when Java is being executed.

By comparison, the *V8 JavaScript Engine* is like the JVM on steroids. It not only runs Java apps in a virtual environment, but it also cleans up after itself to keep your resources from being bogged down by bits and pieces of applications that are no longer in use. In other words, it helps your web-based applications and pages run faster.

Fancy marketing names aside, what does the V8 JavaScript Engine have that enables Chrome to achieve such impressive benchmarks? Three specific features of the V8 JavaScript Engine answer that question:

■ **Fast property access**—In case it wasn't clear, speed is the key when it comes to Chrome and the V8 JavaScript Engine. Since V8 is JavaScript on steroids, it goes well beyond what is offered with the old Java. One of the big differences is that V8 accesses Java properties through hidden classes instead of dynamic lookup, which is a faster way of accessing the properties. From a geek's point of view, there are several big advantages to using this new way of accessing properties. First, it's just so much faster. Second, it allows the use of *inline caching*, which also offers massive performance improvements.

geek speak   *Inline caching* in the most basic terms is a method by which copies of web page code are held at the ready in case you need to use them. For inline caching, those copies are held on the same memory as other programs on your computer, rather than deeper in the system. This allows the pages that are cached to be accessed much quicker than if they were to be pulled from another location.

■ **Just-in-time compilation**—This is used when it comes to code execution. To optimize performance, code is converted before it is executed. For most home users this means that your web applications run much, much faster than before because the code is ready to be executed when it's needed, but it's not just hanging around mucking up the works when it's not.

■ **Precise garbage collection**—In your neighborhood, the garbage collector comes—usually—on the same day each week, likely around the same time, too. This is also the case with the V8 JavaScript Engine in Chrome. Once your "garbage can" is full—in this case, it means memory that is still being used but no longer required in a process—it is "collected," or freed. The V8 JavaScript Engine stops all executions when garbage is collected, freeing up resources for additional processes.

Just to be sure everything is working well, Chrome has another ace up its sleeve: *DNS pre-fetching*. You probably noticed that the most time-consuming aspect of web surfing is the time wasted from the moment you click a link to the moment the page actually loads in your browser. Fortunately, Chrome also realized that this is frustrating to users and decided to do something about it.

DNS pre-fetching is exactly what it sounds like it is—it's when an IP address is fetched before it's called for. Think of it this way. If you have Rover go fetch the paper at a certain time every day, eventually, he might begin to understand that you're going to want that paper. So, rather than waiting for you to tell him to go get it, he picks it up on his own and drops it on the porch steps (instead of leaving it out by the street). Then, when you want the paper, he only has to go to the porch to retrieve it, which makes the whole process faster. It's the same concept with DNS pre-fetching.

When you go to a website, either using a hyperlink or manually using the web browser's address bar, the result is the same. The browser must "resolve" the domain (web address) that you seek; it translates the .com address into an IP address, such as 192.124.1.1. using the Domain Name System (DNS). This process can take time, ranging from milliseconds to several seconds (in case of a timeout).

The *DNS (Domain Name System)* is a translator of sorts that is in charge of assigning domain names to IP addresses, which are the actual web addresses of websites. When a website is called from a web browser, the DNS must convert what you enter into the browser's address bar (www.website.com) into an address that the server can understand (123.456.7.8) before the website can be displayed.

Chrome, unlike other browsers, anticipates your next move. While that sounds mystical, the truth is that this feature is most effective when you contact a website through a page in the web browser and not by manually entering a web address. Here's how it works.

When you open a web page in Chrome, the DNS pre-fetching feature scans the contents of your page for hyperlinks pointing to another website. In anticipation of your next move, Chrome resolves these DNS addresses while you are on the web page, but before you click a hyperlink.

This prevents you from having to wait once you click the hyperlink; the page loads almost instantly. If you have any doubts about the efficacy of this feature, just type "about:dns" in the address bar in Chrome, and you see a full display of time saved using this feature, as shown in Figure 2.6.

Prefetching DNS records produced benefits for 11 hostnames

Host name	Applicable Prefetch Time (ms)	Recent Resolution Time(ms)	How long ago (HH:MM:SS)
c2.com	76	0	52:00
sourceforge.net	116	1	01:01:21
bubbleshooter.net	157	0	03:46:11
aspnetresources.com	233	0	04:02:17
en.wikipedia.org	113	0	04:12:39
www.answers.com	131	0	04:12:39
messaging.myspace.com	138	1	04:21:40
comment.myspace.com	75	0	04:22:24
www.computerweekly.com	153	1	04:54:31
weather.wnct.com	90	0	04:56:17
www.google.com	44	0	04:56:21
---minimum---	44	0	52:00
---average---	120	0	03:47:07
standard deviation	49	0	n/a
---maximum---	233	1	04:56:21
-----SUM----	1326	3	n/a

Cache evictions negated DNS prefetching benefits for 11 hostnames

Prefetching DNS records war not yet beneficial for 295 hostnames

Previously cached resolutions were found for 14 hostnames

Prefetching DNS records revealed non-existance for 1 hostname

Future startups will prefetch DNS records for 10 hostnames

Host name	Applicable Prefetch Time (ms)	Recent Resolution Time(ms)	How long ago (HH:MM:SS)
ad.doubleclick.net	0	37	04:57:23
ad.yieldmanager.com	0	35	04:57:22
media.fastclick.net	0	43	04:57:23
s.tribalfusion.com	0	41	04:57:23
secure.trafficmp.com	0	43	04:57:23
switch.atdmt.com	0	36	04:57:23
toolbarqueries.google.com	0	38	04:56:24
www.burstnet.com	0	44	04:57:23
www.christianchildrensfund.org	0	40	04:57:23
www.mypoints.com	0	0	04:57:24
---minimum---	0	0	04:56:24
---average---	0	35	04:57:17
standard deviation	0	12	n/a
---maximum---	0	44	04:57:24
-----SUM----	0	357	n/a

FIGURE 2.6

Chrome saves you time and patience by resolving anticipated domains before you actually visit them.

The information provided when you use the "about:dns" command includes how long it took to pre-fetch the website (Application Prefetch time) and how long it took to resolve the host when the website was requested (Recent Resolution Time) in milliseconds. The difference between these numbers shows how many milliseconds were saved by using pre-fetching. The other column shows the last time the web page was requested (how long ago).

This feature is enabled by default in the Under the Hood section of the Options window. To enable or disable this feature in Chrome, follow these steps:

1. Open the browser and select the **customization** icon—it looks like a wrench—in the upper-right corner of the page.

2. Select **Options** from the menu that appears.

3. The **Google Chrome Options** dialog box opens. Select the **Under the Hood** tab, as shown in Figure 2.7.

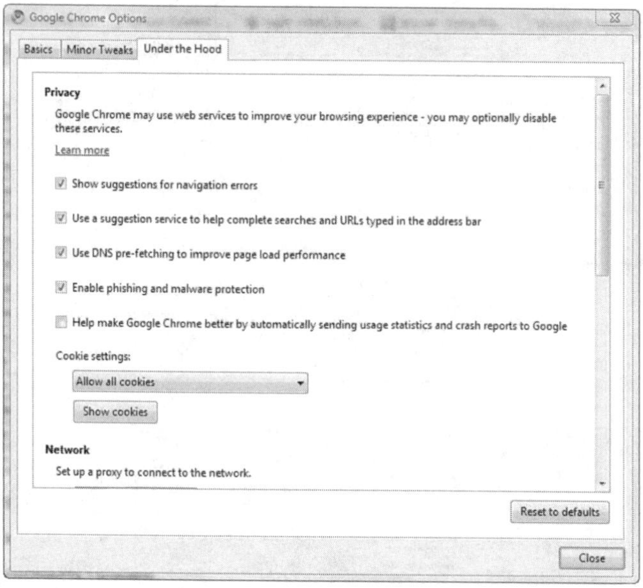

FIGURE 2.7
DNS pre-fetching is enabled by default, so relax.

4. Select the option to **Use DNS pre-fetching to improve page load performance** by placing a check mark in the box to the left of the option. Conversely, you can deselect the option to disable DNS pre-fetching.

5. Once you've made your selection, click the **Close** button in the bottom-right corner of the dialog box to save your selection and return to the browser.

As far as default features go, DNS pre-fetching is particularly helpful, and there's no real reason not to use it. In fact, disabling this option could result in a noticeable difference in the amount of time it takes for a web page to load in your browser. And you won't likely see a noticeable difference in available resources if you're using it.

Share and Share (Resources), Alike

One of the most important lessons we learned as children was about sharing. As we get older, we learn about another important rule—recycling. Recycling is a pretty fashionable—and practical—lifestyle these days. As the old expression goes, "waste not, want not!"

Chrome is no different and, as an open source browser, embraces both the notions of sharing and recycling in its approach to code and libraries. In fact, Chrome uses no less than 25 open source libraries, so you could probably call Chrome the "green" browser. We'll get to much more information about open source and how it applies to Chrome in Chapter 7, "An Open Source Overview."

To be fair, the reuse of code and other resources is a basic tenet of the open source software movement. In other words, by reusing resources, Chrome is simply being true to itself and the movement as an "open source" web browser.

Chrome's decision to reuse resources is beneficial to software developers. For starters, it cuts down on the amount of code that a developer actually has to write. As a resource is used, it gains a certain sense of credibility, which means that developers feel comfortable in the quality of the resource since it has already been used in other projects.

From the user's point of view, there isn't really a tangible benefit to Chrome recycling resources. After all, a user should expect feature-rich software that is efficient and not buggy, regardless of how it is coded (though, admittedly, that's not always what you get with proprietary—or non-open source—applications).

It is also possible that this sharing equals less development time and quicker time to market for releases since there is less code to write. In software as a whole, reusing resources can benefit users when applied to a suite of applications. Reuse, in this example, provides a consistent look across a family of applications that may be comforting to users.

A current list of reused libraries is available online at http://www.catonmat.net/blog/code-reuse-in-google-chrome-browser/. This site, which is regularly updated, provides specifics about each resource, including its path (in the source code) and a description of the resource.

 If you want to know more about the libraries that Chrome uses, you can flip over to Chapter 9, "Spit-Shining Chrome." These libraries are addressed there, and you might find them useful in tweaking the code for Chrome.

Taking Out the Trash Keeps the Browser Moving Cleanly

When you were a child, your mother probably had to constantly remind you of the importance of taking out the trash. How often you take out your "web trash" is likely indicative of whether those admonishments paid off! In the interest of performance, you should frequently clean out your browser's collected browsing data, called the *cache*.

 The *cache* is a collection of copies of websites that you've visited. These copies are stored in a location on your hard drive so that they can be used to help pages load faster if you return to the same website.

The frequency of such spring cleaning really depends on how much or how often you use Chrome. You may even want to clear this data after each Chrome session. If you're a heavy Internet user, your web browser can quickly become cluttered and bogged down by the presence of files in the cache, this leads to a *fragmented disk*, which in turn slows down your computer to a crawl.

The term *fragmented disk* refers to a condition that happens when files are moved around your hard drive. Think of the hard drive as blocks of information. The larger the block, the more you can do with it. Over time, the single large block that is your hard drive is divided into tons of small ones and as programs and data are moved around, large areas are blocked off, or freed up. When the free spaces are all interrupted by the blocked spaces, they become less usable. The resulting disk fragmentation can make large areas of your hard drive harder to access, even though there's nothing on them. Realigning all the blocks of data helps to create larger areas of free space that are easier (and faster) to access.

These aren't the only reasons why you should regularly take out the trash. You must also take into account privacy concerns—for example, if you're using a computer that isn't your own and log on to your bank's website to see your balance, you may want to clear out the browser's cache to completely erase the details of your visit.

Performance concerns are also an important reason to maintain a clean browser. In addition to helping prevent disk fragmentation, cleaning your cache guarantees that you have the freshest data possible. See, a browser draws from copies of cached web pages to speed the time it takes to load a site. So if you visit a site frequently, but don't clean your cache between visits, it's possible that you might not see changes that were made to the site between your visits.

Like all web browsers, Chrome collects personal data as you visit websites. This includes information that is stored directly in the browser, such as where you've been, what you've downloaded, and any stored login/passwords. But web browsers also collect much more than that, including *cookies* that contain personal data (don't worry, not necessarily your name, birth date, and real weight) and are stored on your hard drive.

geek speak

A *cookie* is a bit of information that's added to your browser cache when you visit a website. This information is used to both track your movements while you're on the website that gave you the cookie and helps track your preferences on the site. As a general rule, cookies aren't harmful, though there is some concern that cookies could violate your privacy by allowing companies to track your movements beyond their websites.

When you visit a website, Chrome stores an image of the site as files in the cache (also located on your hard drive) so that it can quickly recall the website when you refresh a page instead of having to contact the remote server a second time to get the data. While caching is a helpful feature, it can lead to both significant file build up in your browser's cache directory and outdated website viewing.

Chrome includes a feature that lets you select which of the aforementioned element(s) to delete and how far back (that day, that week, that month, or all) you want them to delete.

To clear your browsing data, click the Customize icon in the upper-right corner of the browser and then select **Clear Browsing Data.** A pop-up window like the one shown in Figure 2.8 appears. Select or deselect the options that suit your needs by checking or unchecking the box to the left of each option.

Once you select what you want to delete—for example, cookies, history, download history, and so on—and then click **Clear Browsing Data,** Chrome takes control of your browser and deletes the desired files before returning control of the browser.

Unfortunately, this is an area where Chrome comes up short when compared with other browsers. Chrome does not include an option that cleans browsing data for you automatically upon exiting the web browser. This feature would be extremely helpful for us forgetful types who either don't think or don't remember to clear browsing data regularly.

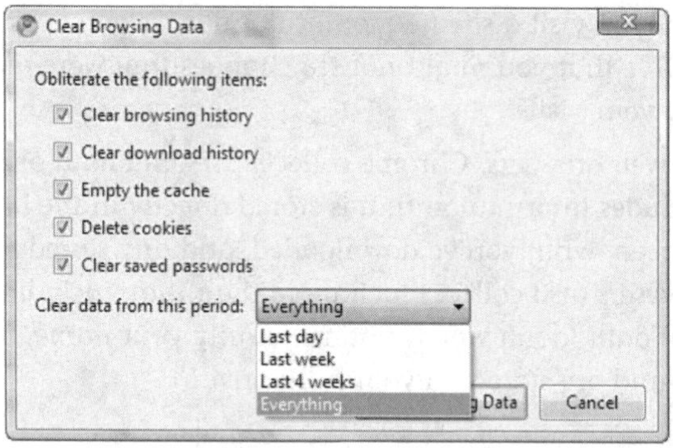

FIGURE 2.8

Chrome lets you take out the garbage without having to get up or get your hands dirty.

Another nice-to-have feature would be selective deletion. If you decide to delete your history of visited websites, it's an all or nothing proposition. This isn't the most helpful proposition in cases where several people use the same web browser and you only want to delete sites that you visited.

Even though these fairly standard features aren't yet integrated into the young Chrome, it's not an excuse for you to get lazy. Make it a habit to manually open the Clear Browsing Data window and regularly take out the trash. Just as living in a clean environment is important to your health, maintaining a clean environment in your browser is important for your computer to keep things running smoothly. Clear out your cache at least once a week.

Searching for the Right User Experience

You are the author of your Chrome user experience. It's up to you to tinker with the features and find a configuration that works for you. Perhaps you won't get to that point, though given the ease of use that Chrome provides, you may end up making Chrome your first-string web browser.

Humans are comfort creatures; we enjoy being pampered. Chrome spoils us with some nice-to-have features that although not unique to Chrome provide an extra level of comfort and ease-of-use to your Chrome experience.

Tabbing Through Life

Like any web browser worth its salt these days, Chrome offers tabbed web surfing. In fact, we even referred to these tabs earlier in the chapter. Tabs allow you to work using several tabs, or websites, within the context of a single web browser window, as shown in Figure 2.9. From a purely aesthetical standpoint, this allows for a much cleaner workspace that uses considerably less screen real estate than if you open multiple Chrome windows.

Individual tabs

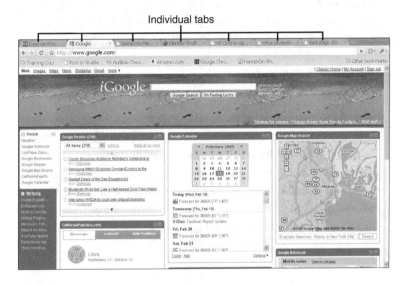

FIGURE 2.9

Keep your desktop clean and your surfing organized using Chrome's tabbed surfing.

Each open tab is like a separate web browser, completely independent of any other open tabs. That means that you can add or close any tab without having an impact on other tabs. This also applies to Chrome features, such as text zoom, which is only applied to the current tab. If you want to zoom in on other text, it must be done individually for each tab.

Another really cool feature of Chrome's tabs is the ability to attach or detach your tabs from the current window. For example, if you open a link from a web page in a separate window and then decide you want to integrate it with other tabs you already have open, you can do that. Just click and drag the tab into the tab bar of the other window. The window then absorbs the tab you're dragging inline with the other tabs in that window.

Alternatively, if you decide there is a tab open that you want to move to a window all its own, click and drag that tab toward the center of the browser window to detach it into its own window.

Finally, you can reorder the tabs in any window using the same click-and-drag movement. Only, you're dragging from side-to-side to reorder the tabs.

The tab functionality in Chrome is pretty useful once you become familiar with how it works. You can use it to organize and reorder the page you're surfing in a way that no other browser allows. So, even though those other browsers have tabs, Chrome's tabs are much more usable.

Surfing Without Being Seen

Privacy is a paramount concern for many people. With the fear of identity theft and other online crimes posing a legitimate threat, some people feel safer about surfing in anonymity. In that respect, Chrome offers an option, though it isn't exactly complete identity protection.

Incognito is a stealthy version of Chrome that opens in a separate window from your standard Chrome window. It masks your identity as you surf. You can recognize Incognito mode by the shady-looking character that appears to the left of the tab, as shown in Figure 2.10.

FIGURE 2.10

This secret agent man means that you're surfing incognito. This feature won't help much if a real secret agent man is watching your Internet habits.

Let's be honest about what Incognito is and what it isn't. The Incognito feature simply means you are incognito to Chrome. Websites visited in Incognito mode do not appear in the browser history, search history, or cookies. Incognito does not protect you from factors that are beyond Chrome's control, such as malware or websites that collect and share information about you. Fortunately, Chrome is clear about what the feature does and does not cover by displaying the message shown in Figure 2.11.

To sum it up, Incognito lets you hide certain aspects of your web surfing habits from your browser and other people who use the same computer. You should always exercise discretion when web surfing, especially when dealing with matters of personal identity or financial data and transactions. Even the best web cloaking features available in standard web browsers may help but are no match for those determined to do things they should not.

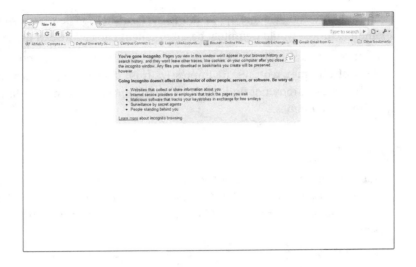

FIGURE 2.11
This information is important reading before surfing Incognito.

NoJokes Internet safety is no laughing matter. In addition to the much publicized threats, such as online predators and fraudulent credit card usage, there are other concerns that you should consider. To help protect yourself against these online, often invisible threats, make sure that you are running up-to-date antivirus and malware software at all times. To be most effective, this software should automatically update regularly and should perform regular full-system scans as well as incremental scans on files that are added to your computer.

It's About the Right Amount of Chrome

Happiness is all about finding the right balance in life. Chrome happiness is pretty much the same thing. Ultimately, whether you use Chrome for your web surfing needs depends on you. This book gives you all the information you need to make an informed decision as to whether Chrome is the right browser for you.

Of course, things in life are rarely black and white, and neither are they when it comes to web browsers. You may find that Chrome is an excellent choice for certain websites, but other websites may require a different browser. Since Chrome is the new kid on the block, it's highly probable that some websites are simply not optimized for use with Chrome. On the other hand, if you are planning on using Google applications, such as the Google search engine or Gmail, Chrome would definitely be an excellent choice for such activities.

In the end, you should use the web browser that is most comfortable to you. Many of Chrome's features are impressive from a technologist's standpoint, but home users may not find much value in benchmark results or inline caching capabilities.

Closing the Door

This introduction to the Chrome web browser offers a little something for everyone. Despite the fact that Chrome is still in its infancy, it provides a number of features that interest both developers/technologists and home users.

Now that you've gotten your feet wet with a general overview of Chrome and its benefits, you are ready to jump in and really learn how to use Chrome. Before you do that, though, you need to get your copy of Chrome downloaded and installed. We walk through that whole process in the next chapter.

Getting Started with Google Chrome

The first two chapters gave you a little background and a little overview; you should have a fairly good idea of what to expect from Google Chrome. It's now time to put that information to good use and get started using the web browser.

Before you do that, however, you need to get a copy of the web browser. Unlike Internet Explorer, Google Chrome is not included with your operating system when you buy a new computer. This chapter is primarily geared toward users who are taking their first steps with Chrome, though there may be a few valuable nuggets for those who are already running Chrome on their computers.

If you're a first-time user, you're going to find all kinds of useful information in this chapter. If you're already past the point of downloading and installing Chrome, you might want to skim through these pages.

A Quick and Easy Download

Chrome is available through online download, like most software packages are these days. The quickest way to get Chrome is directly from the good folks at Google by going to the Chrome website at www.google.com/chrome. Even though other websites may offer Chrome downloads, it is recommended that you download it directly from Chrome's maker, which guarantees that you are not only downloading the latest version of Chrome but also a clean and secure file.

Even though it isn't the most direct way to get there, you can also use the **More** and **Even More** links from the Google home page to access Chrome from the More Google Products page, as shown in Figure 3.1.

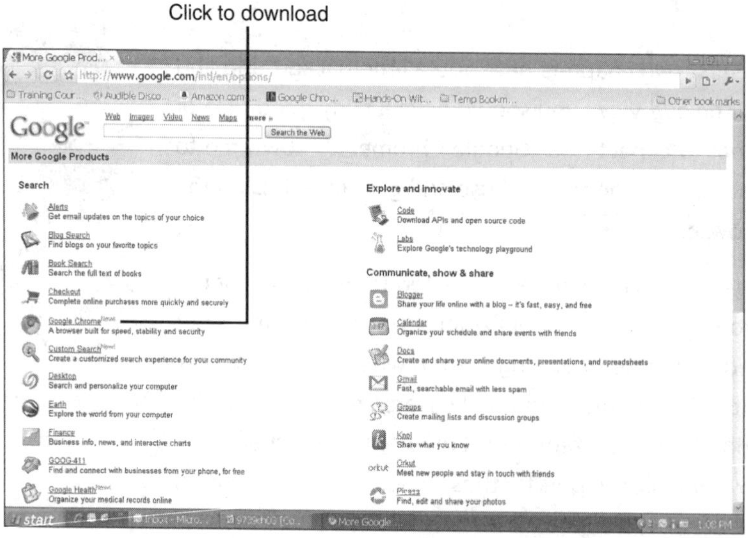

FIGURE 3.1

Chrome is available through several sections of the Google website.

By default, Google detects your language settings based on the location of your IP address. If you want to download Chrome in English, there's no need to backtrack to the main Google website and select Google.com in English.

The Chrome web page allows you to select the desired language for the web browser download from a drop-down list at the top right of the page. Once you select a localized version of the Chrome web page, the information presented switches to that language, and the web browser download is the version for that language.

The actual Chrome web page provides ample information about its highlights and key features via a hyperlink from the main page. Beyond this hyperlink, your only other option is to download, as shown in Figure 3.2.

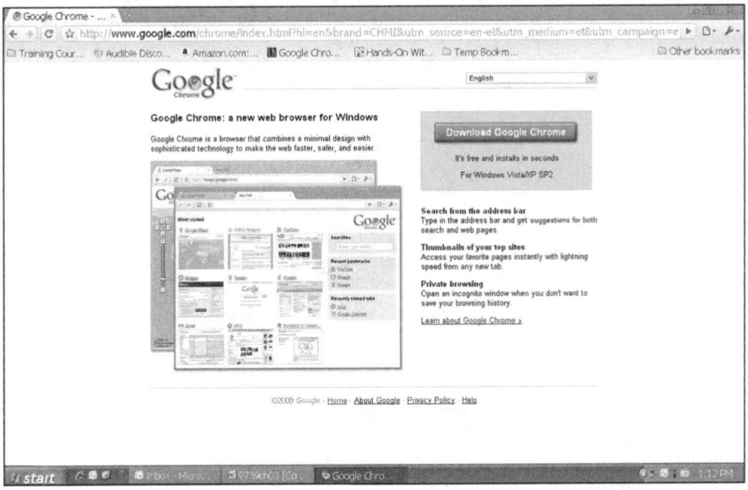

FIGURE 3.2
The Chrome website gives you two easy options—learn more or download.

GOOGLE CHROME FOR THE GRAPHIC NOVEL LOVER

Google's a company known for being progressive. The culture at Google is made up of mostly 20- and 30-something people who are into pop culture and whatever happens to be hip at the time. In part, this can probably be attributed to the (relatively speaking) young founders of the company.

So, it was really no surprise when Google announced Chrome that the explanation for it came as a comic book. The page shown here is just an example of the comic style that Scott McCloud (www.scottmccloud.com) used.

The comic explains the thought process that went into creating Google Chrome, so if you're interested, you can learn more about it (and view the whole comic book) by going to http://www.google.com/googlebooks/chrome/.

Chrome and Your Privacy Concerns

Once the download language is settled and any thirst for knowledge you may have is quenched, you can click the **Download Google Chrome** button. This doesn't take you to the download screen as you might assume but rather to the Terms of Service screen. The terms of service are displayed in a scroll box, but a printer-friendly version is also available and recommended for ease of reading.

It is important that all users stop and actually read the Google Chrome terms of service and not just go straight to the download. A significant amount of controversy has surrounded some of Google's privacy policies. Rather than actually spell these policies out for you, Chrome pushes you off to another website. Regardless, it is worth visiting the current list of privacy policies at http://www.google.com/privacy.htm.

If any of these policies or other terms of service (TOS) are unacceptable to you as a web surfer, click **Cancel**. Just understand that canceling out of the TOS also cancels the download. You can't download and install Chrome if you don't agree with the TOS.

Another feature also is available from this predownload page that lets you take on the role of software tester. If you click the check box to enable this feature, you agree to send usage stats and reports related to any Chrome crashes to Google so that they can analyze this data.

If you do opt to enable this feature, there is no additional work on your part. These stats and reports are sent automatically to Google for you. The Learn More hyperlink associated with this option provides some helpful information for you, which may help you decide whether to enable this feature.

For people concerned about security, know that Chrome doesn't send any personal information that could reveal your identity to Google. However, it does send file and other machine information, such as applications and resources that were running when the browser crashed.

Download and Install Chrome

Once you are satisfied with these privacy and security issues, it's now safe to download the Chrome installer by clicking **Accept and Install**, as shown in Figure 3.3.

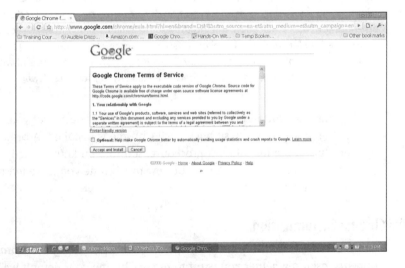

FIGURE 3.3

Once you accept Google's terms of service, you can finally download Chrome.

Chrome saves as an executable file to your default download location (which varies depending on what your current web browser settings are). This file is actually just an *installer* and not the entire installation package, which explains why the file is so small. Once the file downloads, click **Run** to launch the installer.

Yellow Box

If you prefer, you can save the download file to another location on your system. For example, if you plan on performing the installation at a later time you might want to place the file on your desktop or in your My Documents folder. Once the download starts and you're prompted to save the file, just use the **Save In** menu (near the top of the **Save as** dialog box) to select the location where you want to place the file.

You need to have an active Internet connection when you run the installer, as it downloads to a remote server to actually download the Chrome installation package.

geek speak

Many software companies make their software available online using an *installer*. This allows you to download a single executable file that "weighs" a fraction of the entire application size so that you can download the file at a more convenient time. Many installers even keep track of where a download starts so that you may stop a download and resume it at a later time—for example, when there is less Internet traffic—without data loss. Using an installer can also prevent third parties from redistributing an entire software application, forcing the user to still download from the software editor's desired location. The installer is also useful because it's often usable with updates (instead of having to download a new installer) and it's also useful when you change computers, as you're not required to install any additional software.

During this installation procedure, Chrome requires nothing of you. Once you launch the process, simply sit back until Chrome is installed. A progress bar appears during the installation procedure, so that you know exactly where you are in the installation and about how much time you have left before the installation is completed.

Initial Chrome Customization

Once Chrome is finishing installation, a **Welcome to Google Chrome** window appears, asking whether you want to make Chrome your default web browser. You can also customize your settings from this window. Just click the **Customize These Settings** link in the welcome box and a **Customize Your Settings** dialog box opens, as shown in Figure 3.4.

The customization window lets you import existing settings from other web browsers currently installed on your computer. The selection of which browser to import from varies according to what other browsers are installed on your computer.

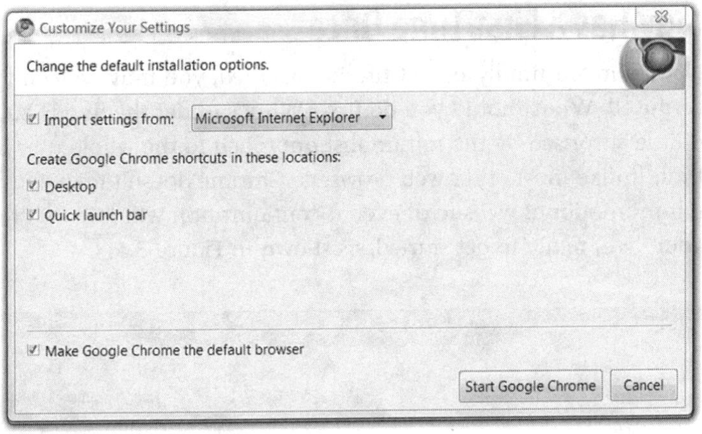

FIGURE 3.4
Get out of the gate running by setting initial browser settings before your first Chrome window appears.

The other customizations are limited and concern where to place shortcuts and whether to make Chrome the default browser. All these options are checked by default, but you can remove the check marks to change any of the settings. If, for example, you don't plan to use Chrome as your default web browser, deselect the **Make Google Chrome the Default Browser** check box.

Once you set these customizations, Chrome completes installation by importing the browser settings as mentioned earlier in this paragraph. These do not include security settings or any aesthetical preferences that you may have set in another browser, but rather any stored usernames and passwords (for websites), your favorites, your browsing history, and any search engines.

At this point, only a single button stands between you and using Chrome. So, why not just click that button and **Start Google Chrome**? Chrome starts up with two tabs open and asks you to sort out the desired search engine to use with Chrome on the first tab. What search engines would Chrome suggest that you use?

Obviously Google is the best option with the Chrome browser, as Google's search capabilities are part of what makes Chrome so much different from other browsers.

The other tab is just information about Google Chrome and what makes it different from other browsers. Take the time to look through this information as it's a great way to help you become familiar with Chrome and to help you get used to navigating in the Chrome user interface.

Everybody Has a First Time Once

Now that you finally have Chrome installed, you may be feeling somewhat confused. What should you do first? What's under the hood? You may even be a little surprised by the minimalist approach to the whole user interface and that, unlike most other web browsers, Chrome doesn't take you to some lame self-promotional website or even a configuration window. You're really just on your own, ready to get started, as shown in Figure 3.5.

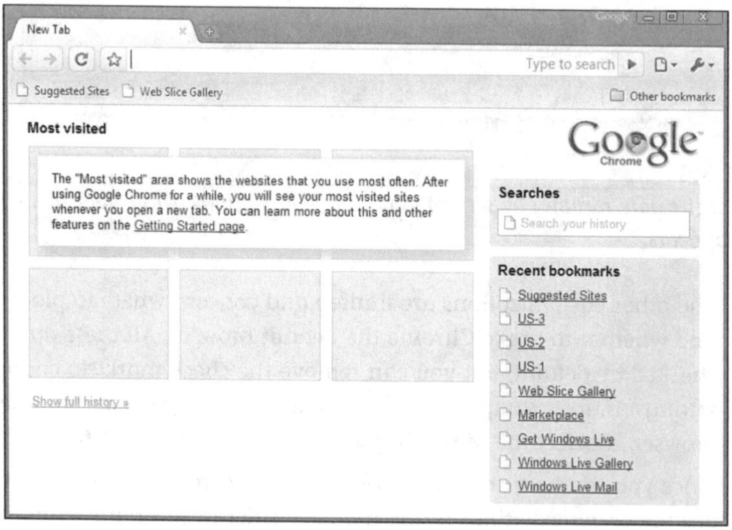

FIGURE 3.5
Chrome, freshly installed, means that you're on your own and the sky's the limit.

Chrome Grows with You

At first, your home page will admittedly be a bit, shall we say, austere. Don't worry; this will definitely change over time, as shown in Figure 3.6. As you surf websites and try out new features, the home page will fill up to include such information as (labeled in Figure 3.6)

- **Most visited websites**—This area takes up most of the home page screen real estate. It includes a thumbnail view of the most recently accessed page of the website. You can simply click the thumbnail to return the website.

- **Searches**—This text box is useful for searching for an article or a page that you visited and is in your history. Note that you can't perform a Google search from this box. You can only search your surfing history.

■ **Recent bookmarks**—This area lists recently added bookmarks. Even if you haven't added any in a while, this list still displays the most recently added favorites.

■ **Recently closed tabs**—This area appears during a single session, where tabs have been closed, without closing the entire web browser. You can recall one of these closed tabs by clicking its title, and it reappears in the web browser in a new tab.

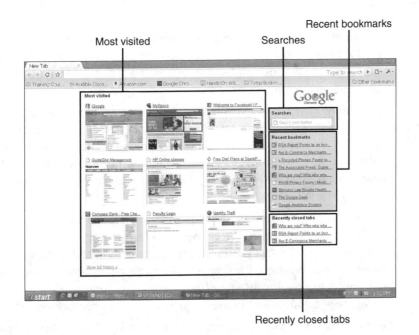

FIGURE 3.6

After you use the Chrome browser for a while, it becomes more useful by placing the links you need right on the main page.

Chrome Page Controls

Once you get past the home page, you may wonder what's next. It's true that the Chrome interface isn't as loaded with text and menus as other browsers, which makes it perfectly acceptable to wonder what you can really do with Chrome besides enter a website name in the address bar.

Almost everything that is to be done in Chrome is done through the address bar—also called the Omnibox—and the two menus—Page and Tools—represented by page and wrench icons on the right of the address bar, as shown in Figure 3.7.

Omnibox   Page menu

Tools menu

FIGURE 3.7

The Chrome address bar and subsequent menus allow you to handle almost everything—in Chrome, that is.

The Omnibox and these other customization and control icons are a discussion for Chapter 4, "It's Everything: The Omnibox (Plus Some)." There's a lot of information in that chapter. But for now, your first time with Chrome should be an exploratory experience.

Spend some time getting to know the web browser. To help you get used to Chrome, visit some of your favorite websites. Do they render in Chrome the same way they appear in other browsers? Do you use Gmail? If so, you definitely want to use Chrome for Gmail, as it is lightning fast compared to performance on other web browsers. In fact, you'll likely make Chrome your dedicated Gmail browser!

Of course, you also want to note any websites that you visit that don't render well in Chrome. Every web browser renders things a bit differently, which may differ from the style sheet defined in the website that you're trying to visit. Like most web browsers, Chrome lets you circumvent some of that by selecting a default font and font size for displaying website content. However, you can't dictate how columns and frames appear, so it really depends on the website.

Remember, most websites (professional ones, at least) are optimized for a specific web browser. That is, they are created with, for example, the Internet Explorer *style sheet* in mind, so that the website developers can guarantee perfect display in a supported web browser. Since Chrome is still new and its share of the browser market is comparably small, there likely aren't many websites yet that are optimized for Chrome.

geek speak A *style sheet*, better known as a Cascading Style Sheet (CSS), is a text file that defines the names of the styles used in a website. These styles are then assigned a set of characteristics, or properties, that define the particular style. This consists of the font or font family used, font size, font color, indentations, and so on. When a website is published online, it uses this CSS file (for example, default.css) to define how the page styles appear in the web browser.

Don't feel bad if you think that you haven't mastered everything or that you don't fully know all the features available in Chrome. Mastering an application, even one like Chrome, takes some time. As you read this book and get acquainted with Chrome's features, you'll realize that the feelings and concerns you had your first time with Chrome are gone!

Point and Click, or Type

Now that the first time jitters are behind you, let's get more comfortable using Chrome. It's helpful to keep in mind Google's goal for Chrome—to get you there as fast as possible. As a user, you can help Chrome meet that goal by finding what works for you.

Humans are creatures of habit; once we find a comfortable way of doing things, we tend to stick with it. Does it matter if there's a better way of doing it? Probably not. If you're just starting out with Chrome, it's possible that you might not have many bookmarks stored. If that's the case, it's time to do things the old-fashioned way: Type it out! Just type the web address into the address bar and press Enter. Easy enough.

geek speak   Most website domain names are accessible without using the "www" prefix. However, this is not the case for all websites. Many websites still require you to use the standard website format—www.*yourdomain*.com. If you don't use the correct format for a website (and there's only one way to find out), Chrome displays an error message indicating that the requested website does not exist. If this occurs, try it again prefaced with a "www."

So, for example, if you want to visit the Washington Post's website, and you know that the web address is "www.washingtonpost.com" the address bar is the appropriate place to enter that address. Once you enter the domain name in the address bar, press the Enter key on your keyboard or click the arrow button immediately following the address bar.

No Joke   Make sure that you pay attention to how you spell those website addresses! Some folks like to buy domain names similar to those of popular websites, only with a spelling error that many people might make. Unfortunately, instead of getting the website you want, you may end up with a website that is quite different—and not necessarily in a good way!

At the expense of sounding terribly lazy, this way of accessing a website is somewhat archaic. Of course it works, but it's hardly in line with Chrome's purpose of getting you there, and getting you there fast. To meet that goal, you're going to want to use the 21st century style of web surfing—point and click.

The easiest way to set up the point-and-click strategy is to use your Bookmarks bar, which is located just underneath the address bar. Once you start adding bookmarks, the Bookmark bars looks similar to Figure 3.8.

Bookmarks bar

FIGURE 3.8

The Bookmarks bar lets you point and click instead of hunt and peck.

Bookmarks in the Bookmarks bar are displayed on a "first come, first served" basis by default. As time goes by, you may find that your surfing habits change. Maybe a website that you recently added gets most of your attention now, but it's also way down the pecking order in the Bookmarks bar. You can always rearrange the order of bookmarks that appear in the bar using the Bookmark Manager, as discussed in the next section.

Bookmark Manager

The Bookmark Manager is, by all accounts, exactly what it claims to be. This is the centralized location for all your bookmarks in Chrome; in fact, it's almost a mini-application unto itself! You can reach the Bookmark Manager by clicking the wrench icon to the right of the Omnibox and then selecting **Bookmark Manager**. A two-panel window displays both the bookmark hierarchy and the contents of that hierarchy, as shown in Figure 3.9.

In Figure 3.9, notice that the left-hand pane displays a series of folders (Bookmarks Bar, Other Bookmarks), recently added bookmarks, and a search feature.

The Bookmarks Bar folder contains the list of websites that are displayed in the Chrome interface in the Bookmark bar just under the address bar. By clicking the Bookmarks Bar folder, the right-hand pane populates with the contents (websites) of the Bookmark bar. From this right-hand pane, you can click a website bookmark and edit its name or web address, delete it, or even add an additional page or folder to the Bookmark bar.

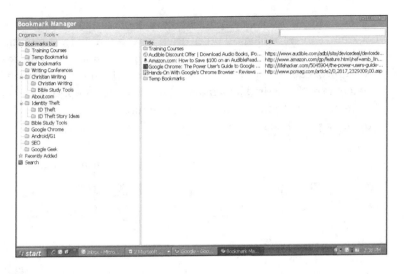

FIGURE 3.9

The Bookmark Manager provides an organized look at your favorite sites and how they are arranged, and ultimately appear, in Chrome.

The next folder in the left-hand pane, Other Bookmarks, is similar in function, only it displays the favorites that don't appear in the Bookmark bar, but rather in the austere menu to the right of the Bookmark bar represented by a yellow folder icon, as shown in Figure 3.10.

FIGURE 3.10

The Other Bookmarks icon lets you display other favorite websites that aren't quite worthy of the Bookmark bar.

The Recently Added folder in the left-hand pane displays the most recent bookmarks in chronological order (from most recent to least recent). The Search button lets you search for an existing bookmark using the text box that appears at the top right of the Bookmark Manager. You can add the first few letters of the desired bookmark, and any matches appear, as shown in Figure 3.11. The Search feature doesn't require any additional work, or even having to press Enter. A few letters should easily do the trick!

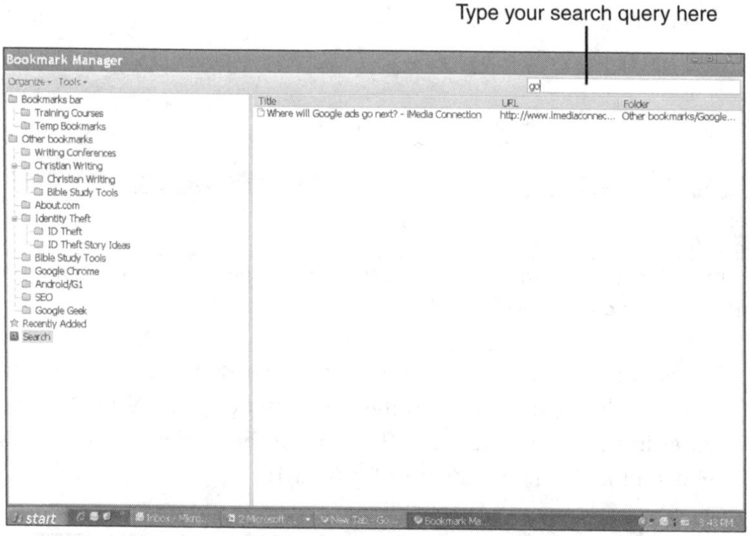

FIGURE 3.11

If you tend to bookmark a lot of websites, you can use the Search feature to quickly locate what you're looking for.

There are two menus at the top of the Bookmark Manager: Organize and Tools. The Organize drop-down menu basically offers the same options as you could get by right-clicking anywhere else in the Manager's panes. The Tools menu, however, is more interesting. From this menu, you can both import and export bookmarks using HTML files.

Your Browser, Your Way: Basic Customization

Bookmarks aren't the only option available to you in terms of customizing your Chrome experience. However, given the minimalist approach to which Chrome adheres, you shouldn't expect to succeed in pulling off an extreme makeover. Besides, when you think of customizing Chrome, it's more productive to think of customizing in terms of making your use easier and your productivity greater, instead of just trying to soup up your web browser. It's important to make your web browser work for you.

For starters, one customization that might make your web surfing easier is to actually display the Home button. For some reason (perhaps in the interest of saving screen real estate), Chrome doesn't actually display this button by default in the interface. This button is still useful, especially if you use your home page as a starting point for surfing to frequently visited websites—all part of the point-and-click strategy.

To make the Home button part and parcel of your Chrome experience, go to the **Options** window, which is accessible from the Chrome Tools menu represented by a wrench. Under the **Basics** tab of the **Options** window, select the **Show Home Button on the Toolbar** option, as shown in Figure 3.12.

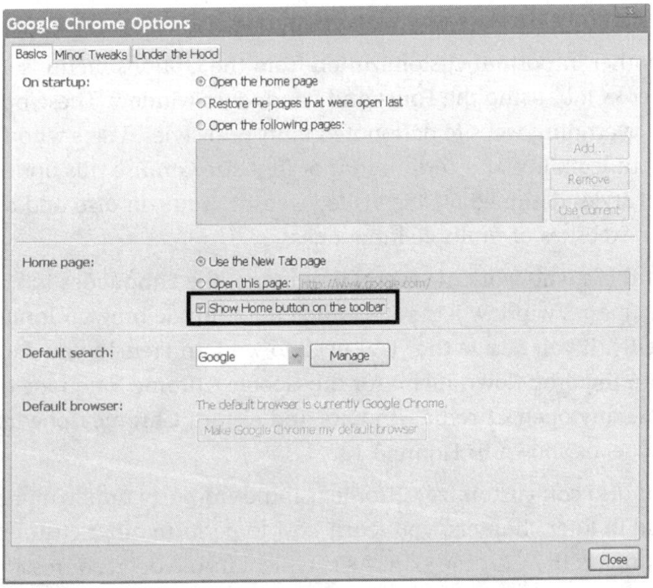

FIGURE 3.12

The Home button doesn't have to show up, but it can make your life easier.

If this is your first time in the Options window, you may want to spend some time getting familiar with its options. Many of your basic customizations are done through this window. For example, the Basics tab lets you set a default search engine, define what Chrome displays on startup, or choose whether Chrome is your default browser. Of course, we cover all the capabilities of the Options window in Chapter 4, so don't worry. You're not missing out; we're just not there yet.

Unlike some competitors, Chrome has an interesting feature in this Basics tab that allows you to go the traditional route and set up a single home page, and you can define exactly what the home page is.

From the **Basic** tab on the **Options** menu, all you have to do is select **Open This Page**. Selecting that option opens a text box to the right of the option where you can type (or paste) the URL for the page that you would like to open as your home page. Just keep in mind, when you enable this option, you lose the option to have the nine most visited sites (and all the other navigational links that are displayed on that page) shown when you open Chrome.

It really comes down to how you work best, but we suggest trying the Chrome way for a while before you go back to the single home page setting. We think you'll find Chrome's way works better.

Another important customization from the Options menu is under the Minor Tweaks tab, using the Fonts and Languages window. These options are helpful for overriding website designated fonts and styles. Users who feel strongly about legibility of a certain font or font size can use this option to override the text styles designed for the visited website. You can also add a language if you visit websites of multiple languages.

For those who work in several languages, the Languages tab of the Fonts and Languages window lets you change the Chrome browser language almost on-the-fly. If you decide that you need to work in French, you can select French from the drop-down menu for the Google Chrome language option. Once you close any open Chrome windows and restart, Chrome appears in the new language, as shown in Figure 3.13.

You also can customize Chrome using third-party applications and resources. And in later chapters, you learn how to perform other customizations, such as changing the Chrome skin. As is typical in the open source community, enterprising users work together to create their own enhancements and make them available to the public. As Chrome becomes more mature and reaches a wider audience, more and more Chrome users will create more and more customizations to make the Chrome experience all the more enjoyable.

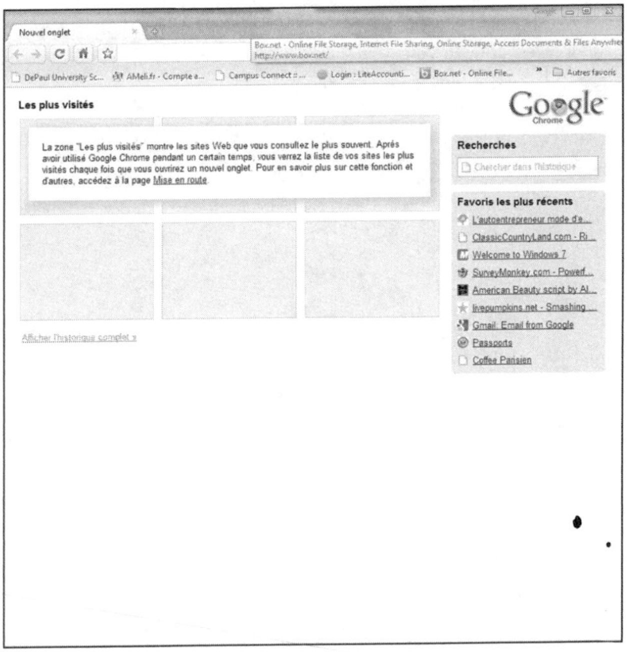

FIGURE 3.13
Chrome speaks almost as many languages as C-3PO from Star Wars.

Closing the Door

Being fast is an important part of Chrome, but it certainly can't be the only thing! Part of Chrome's charm is your ability to tweak it and make it your web browser. Even though still in its early stages, Chrome will continue to grow and become increasingly expansive. As more and more members of the open source community start coding, the sky will be the limit for customizing Chrome!

If you're not the type to worry about how your web browser looks, that's fine too. However, don't forget that a number of the tweaks available in the Chrome Options window are much more performance oriented than they are appearance oriented.

Now that you've had some time to trick out your web browser a bit, let's take a look at one of Chrome's most interesting, yet controversial features—the Omnibox. You also learn a few more customization tricks in the next chapter, so keep reading.

It's Everything: The Omnibox (Plus Some)

When Chrome first became available, it was heralded as being "different." And indeed, it is different. As you've already seen, Chrome was designed from the ground up to be something more than other web browsers. But is there more than just what's under the hood?

Of course there is. You've already seen how the interface is different in some ways, for example, keeping your most accessed websites a single click away. But there's more. Remember in Chapter 3, "Getting Started with Google Chrome," when we talked about the Omnibox? Well, let's take a closer look at that little piece of programming ingenuity.

If It Is Everything, You Should Use It for Everything

In other web browsers, you find an address bar that runs across the top of the browser. You can type any web address there, and the browser loads that website. Chrome has that same address bar, but it has some additional functionality.

The Usual Address Bar Duties

In Chrome, the address bar is called the Omnibox. And in addition to its "usual" duties, the Omnibox doubles as a search box (for the Google search engine by default, of course). It even performs much like the Google search engine interface you're accustomed to by suggesting search terms, as shown in Figure 4.1.

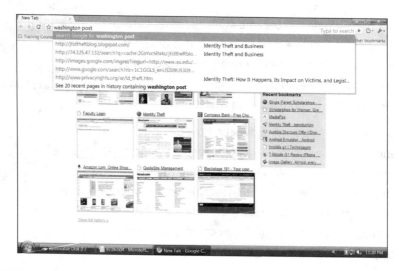

FIGURE 4.1

The Omnibox finds a site for you if you're having difficulties.

Instead of entering a website address, you can enter search criteria, and Chrome displays the search engine results for that particular item. For example, if you want to find the *Washington Post* online and really have no idea what on earth the website could possibly be, just type "Washington Post" in the Omnibox, and it points you in the right direction.

Now, if Google isn't your preferred search engine, you're not stuck using it. To search using a different search engine just begin typing the name of that search engine into the Omnibox. As soon as it recognizes search functionality on a site, a Tab icon appears in the Omnibox as shown in Figure 4.2. That means to access that search engine, just press the **Tab** key. A command opens in the Omnibox for a search of that search engine. Just enter your search phrase and press **Enter**. The search is performed in your preferred search engine, and the results are returned in Chrome.

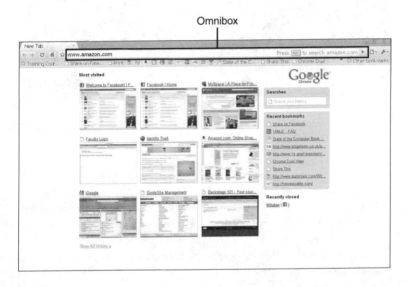

FIGURE 4.2

A Tab icon appears in the Omnibox when a website has search capabilities.

Security Indicators

Improved search functionality is not where the power of the Omnibox ends, however. It's also a tool to help you know that you're surfing on safe websites. For example, if you enter a website that is secured using *SSL security*, you'll notice that the "https" that indicates a secure website appears in green. If there's a problem with the security, you'll see the "https" in red with a slash through it, as shown in Figure 4.3.

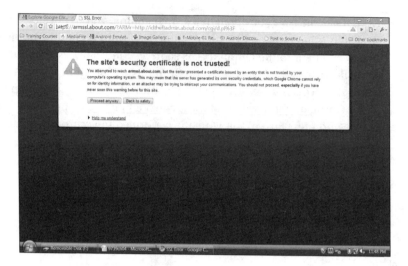

FIGURE 4.3

Chrome's Omnibox alerts you when secure websites are not performing properly.

geek speak

SSL Security stands for secure socket layer security which is a type of encryption that uses secure certificates for authenticating both the person sending the information and the person receiving it. SSL uses an encryption method that includes both public and private keys. Public keys are the method by which the data is encrypted and private keys are the method by which it is decoded. Public keys are more widely available and private keys are available only to the person who is intended to access the protected data.

Because it might be easy for you to miss the shading of the https portion of the web address for the site that you're visiting, Google also includes an icon at the far right side of the Omnibox to alert you to the status of the web page. A lock icon indicates that security is in place and active for the site. The color of the Omnibox also changes to a yellow-gold if security is in place. If there's a problem with the site's security, a caution icon appears in that spot and the Omnibox maintains a white background color.

A Few Other Functions

Another neat feature of the Omnibox is its capability to remember web addresses. This is especially handy if you want to move to a favorite site without opening a new tab to click one of your top nine sites. As you begin typing a web address for a site that you access regularly, the site address will auto-fill.

You don't even have to type in the "www" part of the address. Just type the first few letters of what follows the "www," and as soon as the address is highlighted in the auto-fill you can press **Enter** on your keyboard to load the website.

Chrome loads web pages with lightning speed, and sometimes that makes it hard to stop a page from loading. But if you find yourself in a situation where you want to stop a page before it loads completely, you have that option. While a page is loading, the arrow on the right end of the Omnibox turns to an X. Just click the **X** to stop the page from loading. You can always restart (or refresh) the page by clicking the **Refresh** button, shown in Figure 4.4.

FIGURE 4.4
Control how your web page loads using the buttons on either end of the Omnibox.

When you first start using Chrome, the Omnibox is going to feel a little strange. It will take a few uses for you to become accustomed to the way the Omnibox works, and it might even take a little longer than that for you to change your habits to take full advantage of it.

Once you are used to it and use all the features of the Omnibox, however, you'll find that going back to some other browser is just...uncomfortable.

And Then There Are Page Controls

As good as the Omnibox is, there are still a few more controls that you might want to know how to access. These controls—the page controls—let you use the browser more efficiently. The Page menu on the right end of the Omnibox looks like a page with one corner turned down.

The Page menu is where you find most of the basic controls that you can use on a page, plus a couple of extras. You also find some keyboard shortcuts in this menu. Table 4.1 shows you all the commands available through this menu, what the command does, and what the keyboard shortcut is, if there is one.

Table 4.1   Chrome Page Controls

Command	Purpose	Keyboard Shortcut
Create Application Shortcuts	Opens a dialog box that allows you to create a shortcut to the current page from your desktop, Start menu, or Quick Start bar.	None
Cut	Cut (or copy) highlighted text.	Ctrl+X
Copy	Copies highlighted text.	Ctrl+C
Paste	Pastes copied (or cut) text into the spot where the cursor is located in a document.	Ctrl+V
Find in Page	Opens a search bar specific to the page that you're on (shown in Figure 4.5).	Ctrl+F
Save Page As	Opens a dialog box to save the current web page to your hard drive.	Ctrl+S
Print	Prints the current web page.	Ctrl+P
Zoom	Zooms in to the text on a page.	Ctrl++ (Zoom in), Ctrl+- (Zoom out), Ctrl+0 (Return to Normal View)
Encoding	Opens a list of available encoding types (shown in Figure 4.6).	None
Developer	Opens the Developer menu	None
Report Bug or Broken Web Site	Opens a dialog box (shown in Figure 4.7) that allows you to report a bug or broken web page. Fill in the requested information and click **Send** to report issues.	None

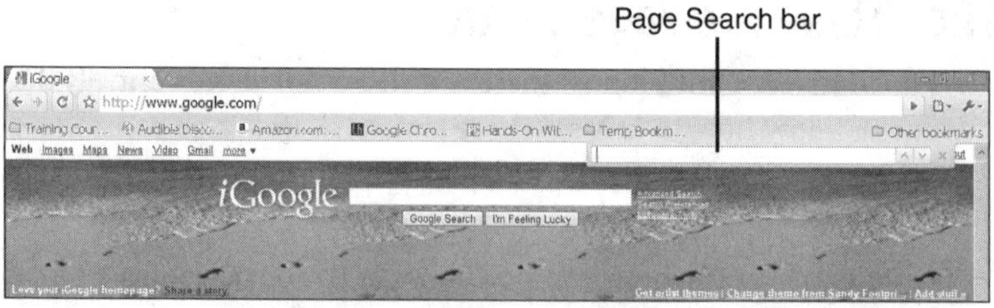

FIGURE 4.5

Chrome includes a search bar that's specific to the web page you're surfing.

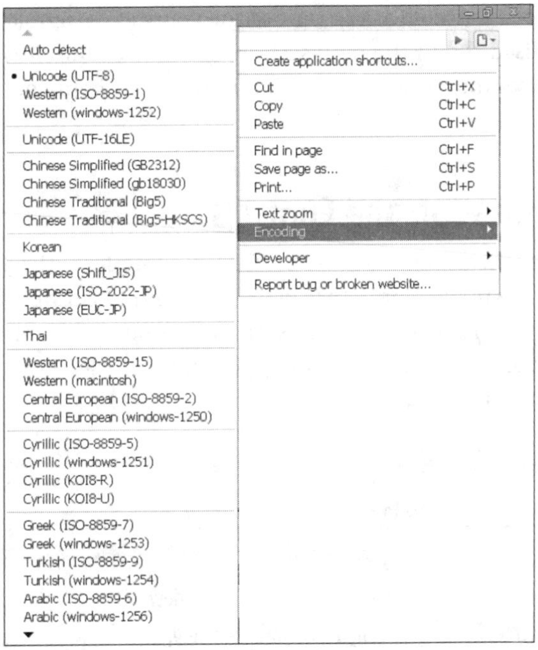

FIGURE 4.6

If your page doesn't render properly, you can select a different type of page encoding to see if that might improve the rendering.

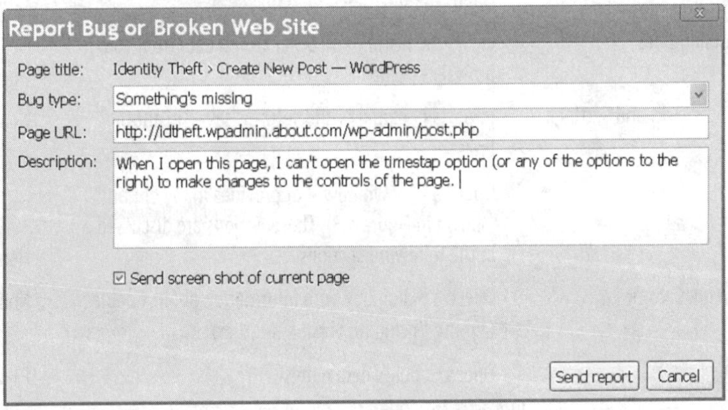

FIGURE 4.7

Report broken web pages or functions on pages that don't work properly so the team at Chrome can continually improve the browser.

Page controls are only one part of the controls available in Chrome. Another menu, discussed in the next section, gives you control over the behavior of the browser and access to additional tools that help you more easily navigate the Web.

More Customization and Controls

The other menu available in the Chrome interface, the Tools menu, is found under the wrench icon. This customization and controls menu is much like the Page menu; you have access to point-and-click controls as well as keyboard shortcuts that make navigation much faster. Table 4.2 outlines the capabilities found in this menu.

Table 4.2   Chrome Customization Controls

Command	Purpose	Keyboard Shortcut
New Tab	Opens a new tab within the browser window	Ctrl+T
New Window	Opens a new browsing window	Ctrl+N
New Incognito Window	Opens a new incognito window	Ctrl+Shift+N
Always Show Bookmark Bar	Enables the Bookmark bar directly below the Omnibox	Ctrl+B
History	Shows your surfing history	Ctrl+H
Bookmark Manager	Opens the Bookmark Manager	Ctrl+Shift+B
Downloads	Opens the Download folder	Ctrl+J
Clear Browsing Data	Clears the history and other stored data from your browser's cache	None
Import Bookmarks and Settings	Imports bookmarks and settings saved in another browser	None
Options	Opens a new window that provides many options (shown in Figure 4.8). These options are discussed in the following sections.	None
About Google Chrome	Opens a dialog box with information about Google Chrome (including version number)	None
Help	Opens Google's help pages	F1
Exit	Closes the browser, including all open tabs	Alt+F4

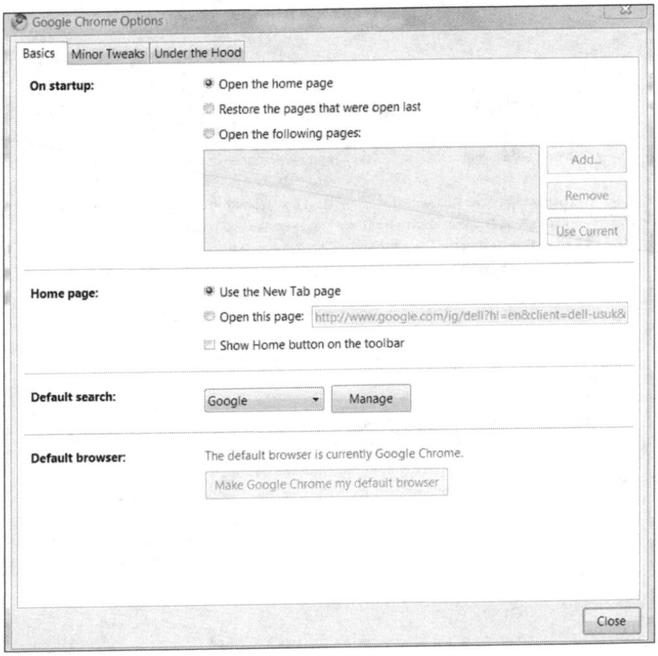

FIGURE 4.8
The Options command opens an additional window of customization options for Chrome.

The Basics Tab

When the Options window opens, it should automatically open to the Basics tab. Four sections on this tab give you options for how Chrome behaves:

■ **On Startup**—This section of the menu gives you options for how Chrome should behave when it's opened. You can choose to have it start on the home page, to restore tabs that were open when the browser was last closed, or to open a list of specified websites. This list includes any websites that are important to you. Just select **Open the Following Pages** and then click **Add**. A new window like the one in Figure 4.9 appears. Select the website you want to have opened, or type the address of the desired website into the text box provided. You can enter as many websites as you want.

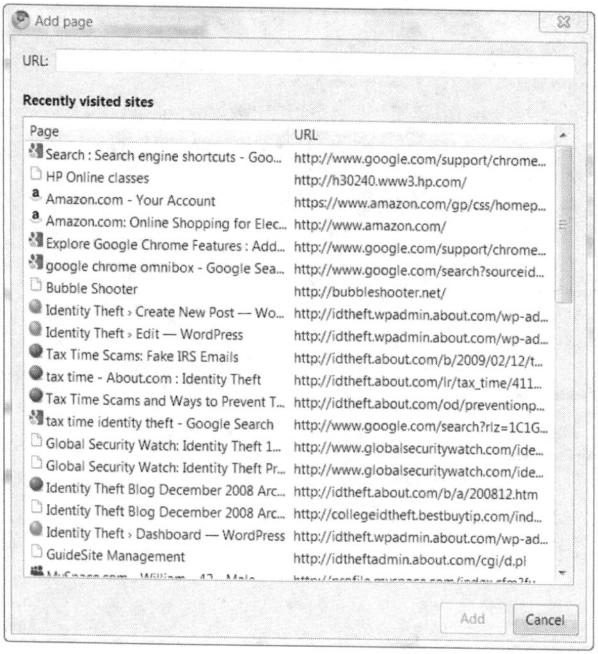

FIGURE 4.9

Add specific websites to open automatically each time you open the Chrome browser.

- **Home Page**—This option allows you to set how you want your browser home page to appear. You can choose the new tab that opens your nine most visited websites, or you can set a specific page to open as your home page. The other option that you find here is the option to show the Home Page button on the toolbar.

- **Default Search**—Google is the search engine for Chrome by default, but you do have other options, and this is where you set those options. You can choose from Google, Yahoo!, Live Search, AOL, and Ask. And if you click the **Manage** button, a **Search Engines** window opens that you can use to add additional search engines to your options, as shown in Figure 4.10.

- **Default Browser**—This is where you make Chrome your default browser. If Chrome is already your default browser, a green notification appears in this section. If there is no notification, click the **Make Google Chrome My Default Browser** button and Chrome replaces whatever browser you currently have set as default.

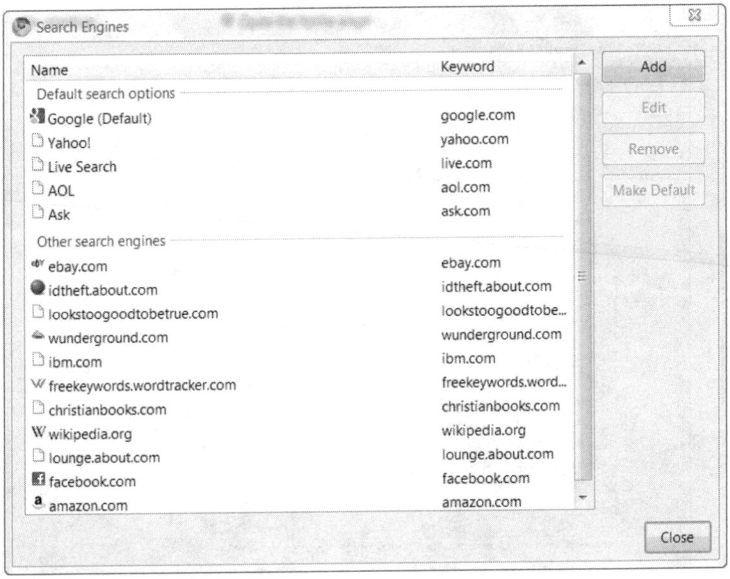

FIGURE 4.10

Even though Google is the default search engine, you can choose the search engines that you're most comfortable using.

The Minor Tweaks Tab

The next tab in the Chrome Options window is the Minor Tweaks tab. This tab provides options that let you set three of the ways in which Chrome behaves. These include

- **Download Location**—This is where you set your download location. By default, Chrome downloads go into a Downloads folder on your hard drive, but you can choose to be asked where files should go each time a new download starts.

- **Passwords**—Here is where you choose whether Chrome should offer to save website passwords for you. You can also view the websites and usernames for which the passwords are saved (shown in Figure 4.11) when you click the **Show Saved Passwords** option.

- **Fonts and Languages**—Use the button in this section to open the **Fonts and Languages** dialog box, where you can manage the fonts and languages that appear in Chrome.

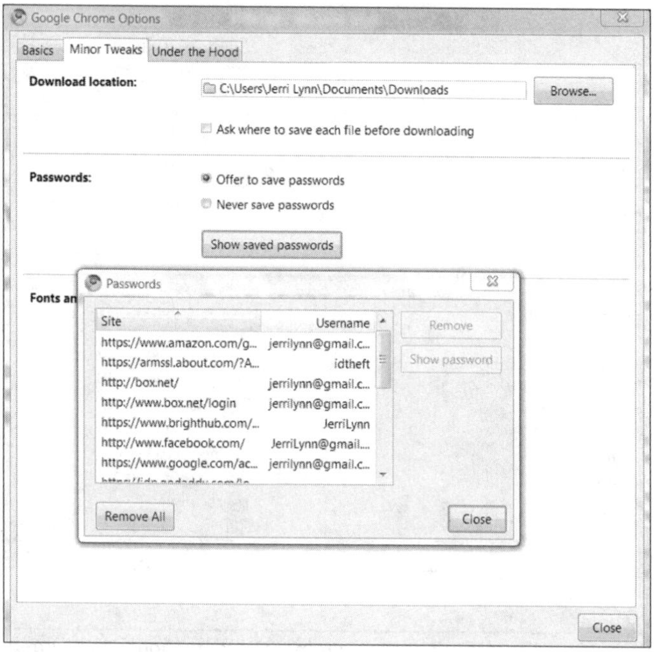

FIGURE 4.11

*Click **Show Saved Passwords** in the Passwords section of the Minor Tweaks tab to see a list of the websites for which you have saved usernames and passwords.*

The Under the Hood Tab

The final tab in the Options window is a bit different from the first two. This tab contains multiple check boxes and additional buttons that allow you to set your privacy preferences, network proxy settings, web content settings, and security settings.

Most of these settings should be left at the default level unless you have a specific need to change them. For example, phishing and malware protection is enabled by default. You can disable it, but then you won't get the phishing and malware notifications and protection that are automatically enabled in Chrome.

Still, if you need to change these settings, you can return to defaults at any time by clicking the **Reset to Default** button at the bottom of the screen. This resets all the option settings that you have changed.

Closing the Door

By now, you've figured out that Chrome is very different from any other browser available today. The Omnibox is one of the most useful and most interesting differences from an interface standpoint. And while the customization and controls are similar to other web browsers, there are a few interesting new features there, as well.

Some other features of Chrome aren't quite as obvious, too. One of those features is unparalleled stability. Since stability has been a major issue with other browsers, you'll be interested to know that the Chrome designers put a lot of thought into creating a browser that's stable under even the worst conditions. Keep reading, because it's covered in all the detail you need in Chapter 5, "Stability on the Net."

4

Stability on the Net

There's really no such thing as stability on the Internet, nor is there a guarantee that your web browser won't crash and burn. If you do any amount of surfing at all beyond just checking email, it won't take too long before you overuse resources or finally open the wrong website, one that has some kind of error or problem on the back end that crashes your browser.

Chrome does, however, take steps to help minimize the hassles of when things go sour between your Internet connection and your web browser. There's no such thing as a crash-proof web browser (or crash-proof PC for that matter), but some of Chrome's security features and behaviors certainly can give you more confidence in dealing with crashes. And it makes crashes that do happen much less destructive to whatever else you happen to be doing at the time.

Consequences of a Crash

Few things are more annoying in personal computing than a web browser crash. Traditionally, a crash in your web browser meant that you would lose everything but the kitchen sink. Literally, it meant that your web browser would shut down, taking with it any open web pages.

If you were visiting a website that required user interaction, such as filling in a form or taking a survey, that information was lost. Even in more recent web browsers that have the multiple tab features, if a single tab crashes, the entire web browser goes down with it.

Crash Management

Fortunately, Chrome offers a completely different style of crash management. To put the new behavior into the simplest of terms, an individual crash is now limited to the affected tab and does not shut down the entire web browser. Should a crash occur, Chrome presents a rather informal way of letting you know, as shown in Figure 5.1. As you can see from this image, you don't even need to close the affected tab. You can simply attempt to reload the page or navigate to a new one.

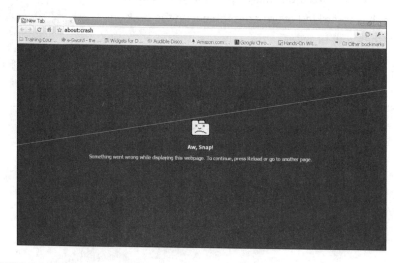

FIGURE 5.1

Chrome has the decency of letting you know when things have run amok, and a sense of humor to go with it.

Before getting to the behind-the-scenes information concerning Chrome's Internet stability, you may want to acquaint yourself with an important feature in Chrome called the Task Manager.

Chrome's Task Manager

The Chrome Task Manager is similar to the Task Manager found in the Windows operating system. You have two options for accessing the Task Manager. You can either press the **Shift+Esc** key combination on your keyboard, or you can go the longer route:

1. From inside the browser, click the **Page Controls** icon.

2. Highlight **Developer** in the menu that appears.

3. A submenu opens. From this menu, select **Task Manager**.

4. The Task Manager appears, as shown in Figure 5.2.

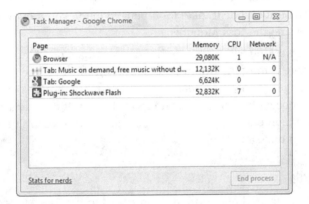

FIGURE 5.2

The Chrome Task Manager lets you take care of any pages that have a resource-eating problem.

The Chrome Task Manager displays the web browser pages currently in use, including tabs and plug-ins. For each page, the amount of memory used as well as CPU and network resources consumed are also displayed in real-time.

If a resource, or page, is consuming a particularly large portion of web browser resources, you may want to consider ending the process. As with the Windows Task Manager, you simply need to click the offending page and then click the **End Process** button to shut it down and free up web browser and system resources.

Unlike the Windows Task Manager, you won't receive a confirmation prompt. The Chrome designers figure if you're ending a process, you're pretty sure that's exactly what you mean to do. If you do end a process accidentally, it's gone. You can either restart that process by closing the tab in which it was active, and opening a new one to navigate back to that page. Or, you can click the reload button and see if the page will reload to what it was before you ended the process.

Once you do decide to end a process, it closes almost immediately. When it closes, the information on the page disappears and you get the "Aw, snap!" message that you see in a crashed tab.

There isn't a hard-and-fast rule about what constitutes "too much" memory or "too many" resources. Common sense dictates when a page should be ended in the interest of maintaining decent computer performance. For example, if you are running a web page that is graphic heavy or uses other technologies such as Java or Flash, and you notice an obvious lag in performance (such as the amount of time it takes for a page to load), you may want to end that page using the Task Manager.

When working with pages in the Task Manager, don't forget that the first, and ultimately, most important page shown on the list is the Browser entry itself. This page also uses considerably more memory than the other entries and cannot be ended using the End Process button. If the memory seems inordinately high based on previous experience, you have to shut down the web browser and start over.

Stats for Nerds

If the basic level of information presented in the Task Manager is not enough to whet your appetite, you can also get **Stats for Nerds** (refer to Figure 5.2). No, this isn't a thinly veiled insult to technologically obsessed readers, but literally an option that Chrome presents at the bottom of the Task Manager. Clicking this link displays more in-depth information via the **about:memory** page. This information concerns the resources that are being used, as shown in Figure 5.3.

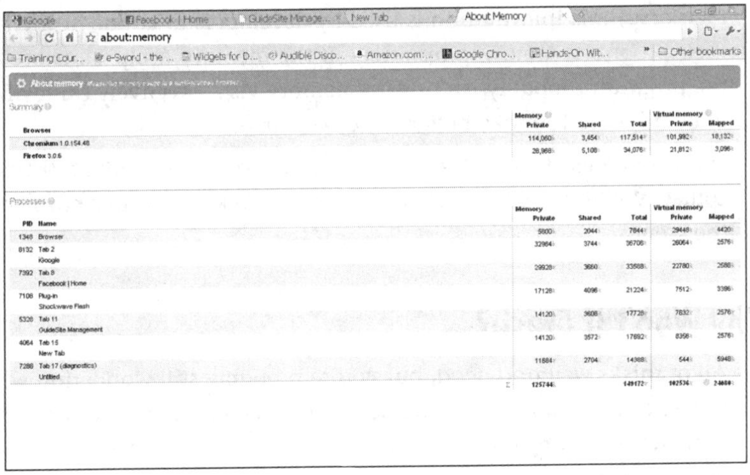

FIGURE 5.3

Stats for nerds are also available if you really need to get to the bottom of things.

Here's a neat feature of the Stats for Nerds option that you might not know: If you happen to be using some other browser in addition to Chrome (I do it all the time, typically Chrome and Firefox), when you open the **Stats for Nerds** option, that browser also displays in the Browser summary section of the **about:memory** page. The information that's displayed in that summary is pretty basic—just memory and virtual memory usage, not process information—but it still might be useful to compare which browser is processing more efficiently.

The information that's provided when you click the Stats for Nerds link includes data about memory usage for different processes and for the browser. So, for example, you can see how much private and shared memory your browser is using or how much processes (like open tabs) are using. Also, there is a measurement for how much virtual memory (both private and mapped) that your browsers or processes are using.

But why do you want to know this information? Aside from being interesting (after all, doesn't everyone want to know whether IE, Firefox, or Chrome is using more virtual memory, private virtual memory, or mapped virtual memory?) this information is used by developers to gauge how effectively their programs are using resources. If the memory usage stats are high, then the program probably isn't using memory very effectively and will likely need to be adjusted to make better use of resources.

For most general users, though, you won't likely need this statistic. Unless, of course, you're a geek like us and just want to know what's happening behind the scenes.

So Why Won't It Crash?

All of this is well and good, but you're probably still wondering what makes Chrome so special that it won't crash easily? And how does Chrome limit the damage caused by a crash to a single tab? The answer is in the web browser's architecture.

The answer is that Chrome uses *isolated tabs*. Each tab, as you saw in the Task Manager, is a separate process, which means that it can act independently of the other tabs in the web browser. Of course, realistically, if one tab is slowing down the entire web browser by causing the web browser to use too many resources, it might have some performance effect on the other tab(s).

geek speak   *Isolated tabs* are essentially separate processes within a web browser. So, when you open a website in one tab and then open a second website in another tab, the two are entirely separate instances of the web browser wrapped in a single interface. (Think of how it used to be when you had to open two separate browser windows. Then smush them together in one browser.)

The processes in one tab won't affect the processes in the second tab, so if you experience difficulties—such as a crash—with one of the tabs, the other can continue in its current state without any information on the unaffected tab being lost.

This feature, while perfect by design, is also effective in reality. Though crashes with Chrome are rare, anecdotally speaking—I've experienced only one crash and at the time of this writing, and I've been using Chrome for more than six months—when it does happen on one tab, additional tabs that aren't affected remain completely operational without compromised performance.

Isolated Tabs Equals Increased Security

There are other advantages to this architecture from a security and performance standpoint as well. For example, from a security standpoint, since each process is independent of other processes, this means that web content in a particular tab subjected to an attack (malware, virus, and so on) is walled off from other tabs. As a result, a compromised tab doesn't run the risk of its attack carrying over to other open tabs in the web browser.

For example, say you've clicked a link in an email that leads to a web page. As that page is loading, you decide you need to access another page since the browser is already open, and you start another tab.

Going back to the first tab, for the purposes of explanation, we're going to assume the email you clicked through was a spoofed message. Although you may not have entered any information on the page that it opened, when you navigate to another page from that page, you could still be in the spoofed web that was created when you clicked through the original link.

Meanwhile, the other tab that you opened is completely separate from this spoofed web. It has no connection to it whatsoever because it's a separate process, even though it's showing in the same browser window. You could reasonably do your online banking in this tab, and it would never be affected by the spoofing and malicious behavior going on in the tab that was opened via the link through the spoofed email.

In short, Chrome provides security.

Using Memory More Efficiently

From a performance standpoint, the isolated process approach limits the number of memory allocations. Memory is allocated for a single tab, which means that it isn't spread all over the web browser, which reduces the risk of *fragmentation* and maintains performance standards.

Fragmentation is a real productivity killer for web browsers and computers. When memory is assigned and unassigned repeatedly in an application, it causes fragmentation. When the memory is unassigned, it leaves little "potholes" in its place, which adversely affects performance.

Does this mean that Chrome is invincible and won't crash? Absolutely not. No software is perfect, and no one should reasonably expect a product in the 0.x and 1.x product line to be as stable or as tested as a product in the 4.x or especially 8.x product line.

For better or worse, the folks at Google really hyped up this feature in particular, which enticed many testers and other people passionate about software to make it their mission to make the Google folks eat their words. Some even found a few errors and flaws. It happens. But that doesn't change the fact that reviewers generally consider Chrome to be far more efficient and far safer than most other browsers.

Like everything in life, a bit of moderation goes a long way. When using Chrome, it's likely that you can successfully operate 15 or more tabs in a single web browser—and a professional user, such as a computer software engineer, may need to do just that. However, realistically, most home users of Chrome will likely use far fewer tabs at a time.

Both home and professional users have the responsibility to keep an eye on available machine resources, including the web browser. You can help manage web browser performance and system resources by adopting the "use what you need" approach; open a new tab when useful, and think of shutting it down when you're done with it.

Still, if you feel the need to go wild opening tabs, have fun! Chances are, you'll have to push Chrome pretty hard to see any effects from it. However, once you get past about 10 tabs, you'll find that the titles on them are hard to read. Around 30 tabs, there is absolutely no way to tell them apart. And it's at about this point that you might start to see some slowing down of the processes in each tab, if they're all working on something simultaneously. However, even at 30 tabs, the slowdown is insignificant enough to make too much of a difference.

Extra Precautions: You Can Never Be Too Safe

Since this chapter is supposed to talk about stability on the Internet, we would be remiss if we didn't remind you of some fairly entry-level information about Internet stability. First, it's important to remember that a web browser is only one line of defense against instability. In fact, Chrome offers a very basic out-of-the-box protection against online threats. Most users will find this level of protection insufficient and will use it in conjunction with third-party applications to maintain the right level of online security.

How can Chrome help you? For starters, it does offer *phishing* and *malware* protection from the Options menu, as shown in Figure 5.4.

Unfortunately, there aren't any configuration settings, or even feature descriptions beyond that simple check box. Chrome keeps an eye open for websites that may be known for phishing, and should you try to access those sites, a red warning page appears, letting you know that the site is suspected or known for phishing activities. The same is true for other known malware applications on the Web.

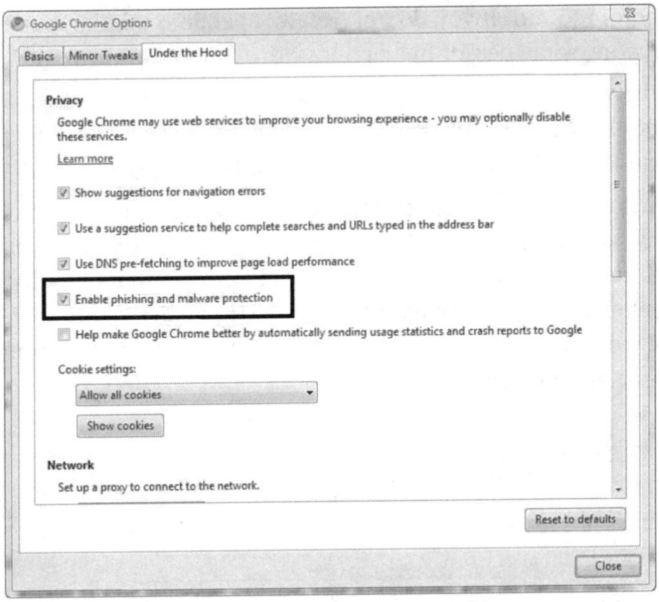

FIGURE 5.4

Chrome can add some phishing protection for you, leaving you time to work.

geek speak

Phishing? Malware? How can I keep track of all these threats? *Malware* is a more generic term used for software designed to gain access to your computer (without your knowledge) and do harm. This can be the classic computer virus, a Trojan horse, spyware, and so on. Whatever form malware takes, it is never good.

Phishing refers to an online scamming technique whereby an ill-intended person sends a bogus email pretending to be from a large or famous website in the hopes of getting you to reveal personal information. For example, an email may claim to be from the World's Largest Bank and that you need to confirm your personal details by clicking the link in the email. The link is often a different or a spoofed web address that snares you in and gets your information once you go for the bait.

If you want more reassurance with respect to malware protection, consider running a third-party application to keep an eye on your entire system. It's feasible that Chrome may not be the only web browser that you or other users use on your machine, and it's not safe to assume that all web browsers offer malware protection.

In addition to malware protection, it's good sense to run both antivirus protection and a firewall. Most computers today come with at least a trial antivirus program to run. If you do not feel like spending a lot of money on antivirus software, some decent free options are available online.

A firewall is also a wise option, even if you aren't a "techie." If you are running the Windows XP operating system or later, an out-of-the-box firewall is included, which adequately covers your basic needs.

One last tip for network stability is to keep an eye on the color of your web browser's Omnibox. In Chrome's case, the Omnibox turns yellow if you visit a website whose content is secured. You'll also see that a padlock appears on the right end of the Omnibox, as shown in Figure 5.5, along with the name of the security certificate holder, and the "https" at the beginning of the address shows up in green.

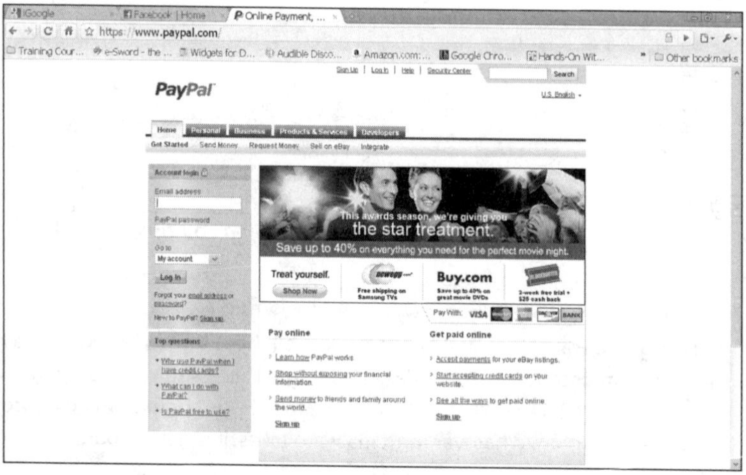

FIGURE 5.5

Chrome lets you know if the site you want is truly safe to visit.

If you click the padlock that appears on the right-side of the Omnibox, you can find out important security information, as shown in Figure 5.6.

The Security Information window confirms the identity of the website as well as the issuer of the SSL certificate (VeriSign, Thawte, and so on). This is important, because websites where the security certificate issuer can't be verified or where the security certificate might be expired aren't necessarily safe places for you to share your personal information.

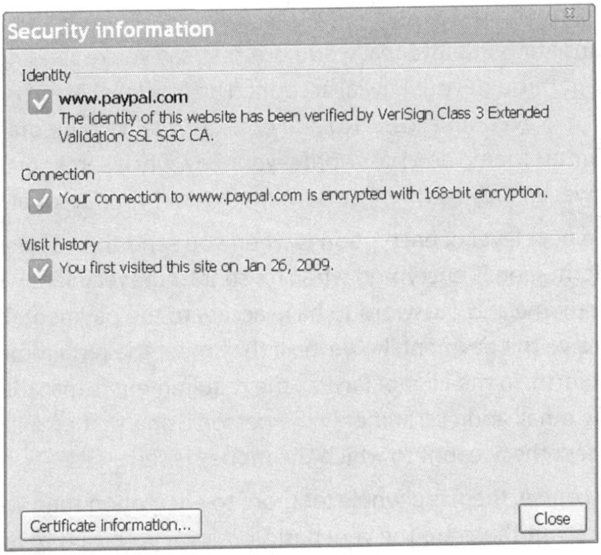

FIGURE 5.6
Before visiting a secured website, find out what's behind it.

The next thing you'll see in the window is a connection verification. This lets you know what website the browser thinks you're connected to—which is important if you're visiting a site that appears to be one site but is actually another (called spoofing)—as well as what encryption strength the site has. Encryption strengths can be a bit confusing, but you certainly don't want to share your information on a site that has anything less than 128-bit encryption; 168-bit encryption is even better.

UNDERSTANDING WEBSITE ENCRYPTION

Website encryption is based on a cryptographic method for hiding data in which data cannot be "seen" without a key to unlock it. Now, technically, you could see the data, but it would make absolutely no sense to you, because it's written in binary code, which is made up of all 1s and 0s.

So, when you include user encryption on a website, you essentially hide the data from everyone until someone comes along that has a special key that can unlock that data. At that point, that person can see the data.

Translating this into real world use, let's say you're sending a PayPal payment through your PayPal account. The first level of encryption is going to be your account access. No one can see your account unless they have your username and password—your key. Once someone has that key however, they can view everything that's in your account.

The next level of encryption is when you send the payment. The payment information is encrypted when it's sent to the recipient who must enter a username and password to have access to the payment. They can only receive the payment, however, if they meet the requirements that you've set forth. In the case of PayPal, the requirement is that they possess a specific email address, and only the person using that email address can access the account to which the money is sent.

Of course, there is a whole lot more to encryption than we can go into here, but these are the very basic, basics. If you want to learn more about encryption, a good starting point online is: http://www.inet2000.com/public/encryption.htm.

Finally, the window indicates whether you've previously visited the website.

If a website has an invalid or expired certificate, Chrome does not load the web page until you give it explicit permission. The Chrome Options page has a feature in the **Under the Hood** section labeled **Check for Server Certificate Revocation**, which allows you to display the Omnibox in different colors in cases of anomalies (such as invalid or expired certificates).

If you are not sure about the security of websites that have certificate issues, it's best to err on the side of caution. However, do keep in mind that not every website that has a certificate issue is necessarily a problem website. Just use caution and don't take any unnecessary risks.

There's No Little Black Box in the Browser

Most everyone has heard of the black box recorders on airplanes that are responsible for noting all communications between the pilots and the control towers, as well as vital airplane flight data. Of course, these black boxes only seem to work effectively in a limited number of cases, which is the perfect segue into a potentially useful feature in Chrome!

Chrome has its own sort of limited black box recorder built-in. Here's how it works: In the event that Chrome crashes and ultimately shuts down, it can automatically restore the session open just prior to the shutdown. If you're familiar with the Firefox web browser, you know that it also has a similar feature.

This feature, like so many others, is available from the Chrome Options window.

1. Open the browser and click the **Tools menu button** (which indicates the customize and controls menu).

2. In the menu that opens, select **Options**.

3. Make sure you're on the **Basics** tab and then select the **Restore the Pages That Were Open Last** radio button from the On Startup section, as shown in Figure 5.7.

4. Click **Close**. Then close and reopen the browser for the new setting to take effect.

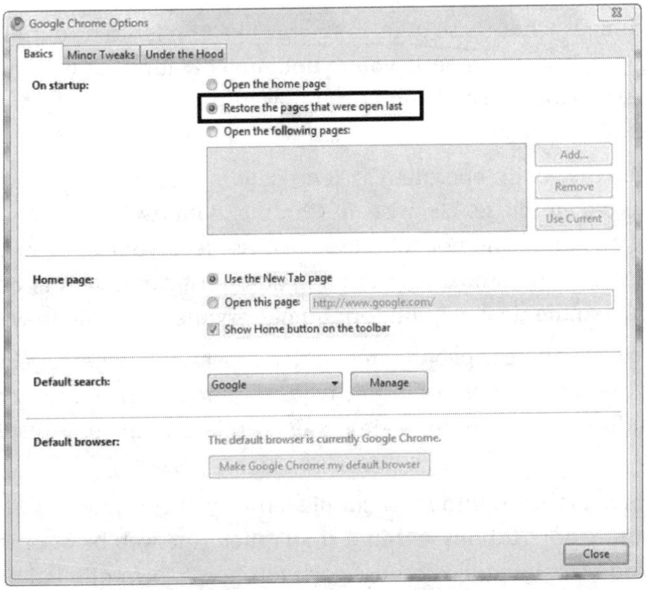

FIGURE 5.7
Chrome can sort of get your lost work back.

It is important to keep in mind that this is not an option that can be applied after the fact. If your web browser crashes, you cannot raise the dead by setting the feature and expecting Chrome to bring back your websites. Rather, it's a preventive measure that you must enable ahead of time to avoid pulling out your hair should Chrome crash. It's easy to overlook this feature when you start working with Chrome because it's presented as a setting that is applied when you open your web browser (akin to defining what the "home" page is) and not necessarily a security issue.

Nevertheless, this feature isn't necessarily one you should depend on with your life. As Chrome is still in its early releases, admittedly, the feature doesn't always work. If you are working with a website that is of particular interest to you, the safest way to ensure you can get back to it is to bookmark it.

Also, an equally reliable method to recall lost work is to enter the domain name in the Omnibox. Until you clear out your cache, the visited website is still available in the Omnibox. Even if you don't recall the exact URL of the desired website, you can probably find the name of the site in the Omnibox or history by typing just a few letters.

Weaving a Multithreaded Web

Chrome is what those of us in the biz like to refer to as a multithreaded web browser. If you're a geek, you're undoubtedly familiar with the concept of multithreaded architecture. Until now, this concept was best exemplified in operating systems.

In the case of an operating system, data is used in groups or clustered and not collected en masse. Likewise, in Chrome, data (websites) are used in groups (isolated tabs) and not collected en masse (everyone else), as illustrated in Figure 5.8. In both cases, offending data that can't seem to behave itself is shown to the door, without bringing everyone down along with it.

Of course, there is debate among developers as to whether Chrome is doing anything revolutionary in this regard. After all, operating systems that use multithreads use multiple processors, while Chrome uses just a single processor.

To break it down into more simple terms, you can think of Chrome tabs as separate applications within a single shell (the web browser itself). The comparison can be made because each tab has its own allotted memory, just like Microsoft Word and Adobe Acrobat do when you run them under Windows.

To go one step further, each tab is thus its own thread. Why is this important? Even though the Web has gone further than many of us imagined possible as little as 15 years ago, plenty of website developers still haven't the foggiest idea of how to code or write memory-efficient web-based applications. The end result is that many websites end up using more memory than they really should, to the detriment of your other tabs.

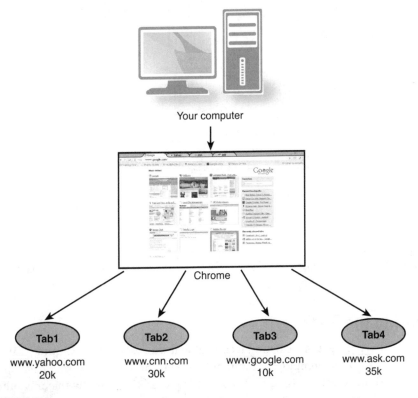

Your computer

Chrome

| Tab1 | Tab2 | Tab3 | Tab4 |

www.yahoo.com www.cnn.com www.google.com www.ask.com
       20k   30k   10k   35k

FIGURE 5.8

Here's a basic interpretation of what multithreaded architecture means to Chrome.

You can see proof of Chrome's multithreaded architecture when you open the Windows Task Manager. By way of comparison, open up an instance of Firefox and open up a couple of websites in separate tabs. Then, launch Chrome and call up a few websites in separate tabs.

Once you open up the Windows Task Manager, you can see that Firefox is displayed as a single resource in Task Manager, while Chrome has as many entries as there are tabs currently open, as shown in Figure 5.9. This demonstrates the independence that each tab enjoys.

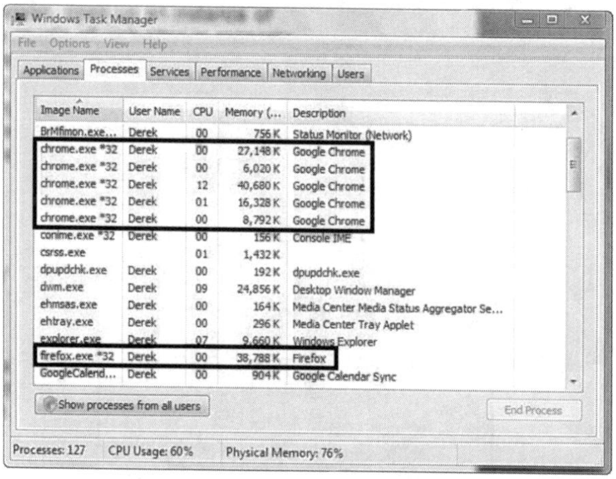

FIGURE 5.9

If you use three tabs in Chrome, the Windows Task Manager shows you multiple Chromes.

Closing the Door

One of the most exciting technical features available in Chrome is its isolated tabs, which employs a commonly used technique in software development. It's somewhat surprising that Internet Explorer 8 is currently the only other browser that uses that capability.

One major complaint against software developers is that they tend to develop applications from a developer's standpoint, disregarding what the public wants in an application. If, for some, the isolated tabs capability is one of those instances, then it's one that will definitely benefit the public.

A web browser can only offer a certain level of security; it's also up to website developers to offer a quality website in terms of design and security. Chrome's ability to shut down offending websites without shutting itself down shows it to be a strong competitor in the web browser field from its first release.

Again, it's important not to rely totally on your web browser for Internet stability. Chrome is ultimately designed to surf websites, not provide enterprise-level Internet security. Ultimately, it's up to the user to pick the right tool for the right job.

Safe Browsing on a Threatening Web

I t's a rough world out there! One of the biggest mistakes you can make when you're working or playing online is to think that the Web is some innocuous place, where everyone has the best intentions. That's why it's extremely important to not only know what threats exist on the Web, but also how to mitigate the risk of falling victim to one of them.

Chrome can help you reduce the risk of some online threats, as you read in Chapter 5, "Stability on the Net," but much more can be done on both a technological level as well as a personal behavior one. In this chapter, you learn more about these threats and even more about how to make your Chrome experience positive and safe.

It's Not If, It's When You're Attacked

As you've already been warned, one of the worst online attitudes to adopt is one that falsely allows you to believe that nothing bad can happen to you. Another equally bad idea is to keep on running with that belief and not use any of Chrome's security features or a third-party application to reduce risk.

A safe bet in computing is to always believe that someone or something is after you. Of course, that may sound like paranoid talk, but as the old saying goes, it's not paranoia if it's true. Take a look at the statistics surrounding Internet crimes found on the Consumer Fraud Reporting website (http://www.consumerfraudreporting.org/internet_scam_statistics.htm), and you'll be completely convinced that everyone is at risk online.

Every time you visit a website, you open yourself to all kinds of online threats, such as malware, viruses, Trojan horses, spyware, and so on. Even if these technological misfits aren't singling you out specifically, they don't need to. An attack that snares just one, targeted Internet user isn't all that useful to most of those who seek to use the Internet to do harm to others. Most online scams are set to cast a very wide net, targeting anyone and everyone not careful enough to avoid falling into their traps.

To be honest, much of your online threat profile also depends on what kind of websites you are visiting. It's unlikely that you'll expose yourself to anything more than a cookie (which is something that you can control anyway by blocking them in your web browser) when you visit the website of, for example, a major news organization or a huge online book and music store.

If you visit riskier websites, such as ones that offer *peer-to-peer* conduits or that allow anyone with an account to post accessible content, you run the risk of downloading uglier items. These websites are great ways to download viruses or Trojan horses onto your computer.

Given the amount of traffic such websites generate, there's no point in telling you not to visit one. If you do, however, make sure your computer has all the necessary online protection it needs so that you don't spend a weekend having to reformat your hard drive and then rebuild your computer.

6

Peer-to-peer software allows you to share files stored on your computer with anonymous users all over the world through software called *torrents*. Through websites that act as online directories or catalogs, you can download a torrent that connects to other computers on the network that make any file available for download through the peer-to-peer client software.

Since this process is largely anonymous, there's no way of knowing whether the files available from others are corrupt in any way (virus, Trojan, spyware). These files, if not checked using malware and antivirus software, present a substantial risk to the well-being of your computer.

With all this information in mind, it's worth a reminder from Chapter 5 that the use of Chrome's security features (albeit limited) and third-party applications are crucial to browsing safely. You can think of each component of protection as a layer of chain mail in your online suit of armor. Each piece of that armor represents a layer of protection that you should add to your computer:

- **Antivirus software**: Antivirus software protects your computer specifically from viruses that circulate the Internet. Viruses can be delivered to your computer through emails, even when you do something as simple as log onto a website. You should have an antivirus software active and updated on your computer at all times.

- **Sandbox**: Sandboxing is a method of running computer code separately from the rest of your system. In a browser, sandboxing is the technique that's used to create separate tabs for each instance of a web page in your browser. Each tab represents a separate process that's unaffected by and that does not affect other processes.

- **Firewall**: Think of a firewall as a perimeter around your Internet connection. It provides a gateway through which all data has to pass when leaving and arriving at your computer. If something isn't suppose to get through (like a virus or other malware), the firewall cuts it off before it passes the perimeter.

- **Anti-malware software**: Antimalware software works like antivirus software, except that it specifically targets malware—Trojans, spyware, and other nasties—from infecting your computer. Anti-malware doesn't look for viruses, though, so it should be used in conjunction with antivirus software.

Chrome Saves the Day?

Chrome, like most web browsers, only offers limited built-in protection against online threats. For starters, it offers a generically titled "phishing and malware protection" that you can enable from the Options window with a simple click. Unfortunately, Chrome doesn't really detail what those options are, although you might guess that the web browser is keeping its eyes peeled for any websites that either try to get you to provide sensitive information to a suspicious website or try to plant suspicious files on your computer.

Chrome also offers other security features that are important enough for you to consider. Like almost everything else, these features are available in the Under the Hood tab of the Google Chrome Options window, as shown in Figure 6.1.

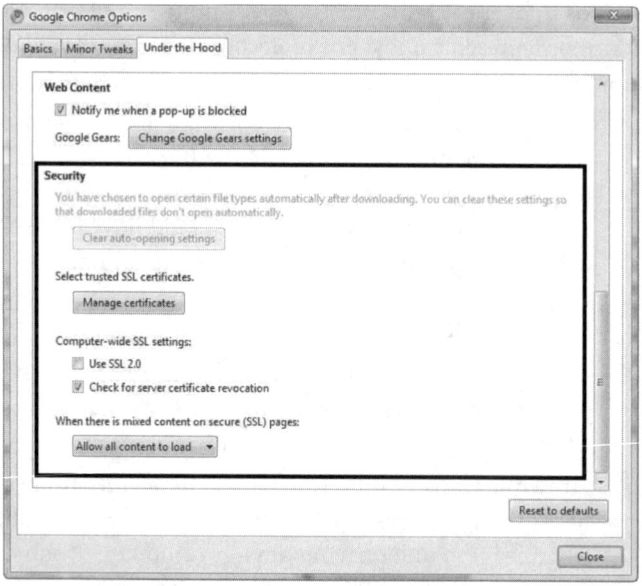

FIGURE 6.1

Malware isn't your only security issue; Chrome also lets you handle other security issues, such as SSL and auto-opening.

Chrome breaks down the security options into two categories; first, you can work with your auto-open options, and then you can configure how Chrome works with SSL (Secure Sockets Layer).

In the interest of convenience, Chrome lets you automatically open certain types of files immediately after a download is completed. The advantage is that you do not have to manually locate a file and then start the installation procedure or lose precious seconds opening the file in another application.

The security threat comes in when downloaded files are not automatically analyzed on-the-fly by any third-party antivirus software. In this regard, Chrome has no control over what happens when the file is opened. If you configured an antivirus program to analyze all downloads, it scans the file for you before Chrome makes it available to open.

It doesn't take a genius to imagine what happens if you do not have such a configuration enabled and Chrome automatically opens a file that happens to be infested with viruses or other unpleasant things. It also doesn't take a lot of time for the damage to be done once you do open an infected file.

If you have designated any file types as auto-opening file formats, it's perfectly fine to have second thoughts about it. Auto-opening files, which can be just about any type of file that you download, can be a tremendous convenience. For example, I have my computer set up so that Microsoft Word files automatically open when I download them. However, if I were to open a Microsoft Word file that was infected with a virus or other type of malware, then that malware or virus would be automatically installed on my computer when the file opened. Fortunately, you can change the option at any time:

1. From within the open browser, open the **Tools** menu (indicated by the wrench icon) and select **Options**.

2. When the **Google Chrome** Options dialog box opens, select the **Under the Hood** tab.

3. Scroll down the page that appears there until you find the **Clear Auto-Opening Settings** button. You can end those auto-opening associations by clicking this button.

4. When you're finished, click the **Close** option to save your settings and return to the browser.

Again, if you take the necessary precautions, this is a perfectly safe feature that may be of benefit to you.

Secure Sockets Layer

The next set of security options in the Under the Hood section of the Google Chrome Options menu involves *Secure Sockets Layer (SSL)*, which is a protocol for secure online connections. SSL can take on several incarnations; for example, you may use SSL to connect to your email account for downloading and sending email. This lets you handle your business with complete confidence. Of course, it also has other useful purposes, such as when it comes to working with certificates.

Secure Sockets Layer (SSL) is a security protocol that encrypts data that's transmitted over the Internet. That includes data transmitted through email as well as data that you enter into forms online.

Many websites (especially those that require a certain level of security, such as those that allow online transactions, account access, and so on) use SSL certificates to establish a relationship of trust between the website and your computer.

When you visit a website that is secure, it sends a "trusted" SSL certificate to your computer (web browser) that shows its credentials, which in turn allows Chrome to connect to the website securely. You can think of this certificate as a secure ID, much like you would use to access a secure location, such as a military base, a restricted airport zone, and so on.

The browserwide settings in Chrome allow you to use the *SSL 2.0* protocol, instead of the default SSL protocol. Frankly, this is an unusual option to provide, as SSL 2.0 is a decidedly outdated version (SSL 3.0 is a more commonly used protocol).

In fact, Chrome doesn't even indicate what version of SSL the web browser uses natively. If you are not sure whether you should be using SSL 2.0, you may want to err on the side of caution and leave this option unchecked (which is also its default setting).

SSL 2.0 is a security protocol supported by Chrome. The most recent SSL version is 3.0, which should give you an indication of how old it really is. There are a number of compelling reasons not to enable this feature, notably with respect to security itself! SSL 2.0 suffers from several well-known security issues, such as vulnerability to attacks, and also has a weakened MAC structure. As noted, it's better to leave this alone unless you are certain it is supported.

Security Certificates

The other browserwide option in the Under the Hood section of the Options tab allows you to check for server certificate revocation. As discussed previously in Chapter 5, this feature allows the Omnibox to appear in different colors in cases of anomalies (such as invalid or expired certificates). To be perfectly honest, not every certificate anomaly is necessarily a sign of evildoing.

For example, it's possible (though still careless), that a website owner didn't renew the SSL certificate in time and it lapsed. It's also possible that the website owner tried to implement an SSL certificate to prove authenticity but didn't know what he was doing and instead raised a red flag. Such mishaps are not uncommon, but they do require you to either take a risk and hope that the site is secure, or have to worry about why the site wasn't able to implement an SSL certificate properly.

In either of these scenarios, the certificate is revoked by the certificate authority (VeriSign, Thawte, and so on) and is no longer a trusted certificate. You can still connect to the website, but you won't be able to do so with the same confidence as when connecting with a trusted certificate.

It is recommended that you leave this option enabled in Chrome, so that you have a better level of understanding with regard to the state of security of the websites that you visit.

When you are visiting a website securely over an SSL connection, not all the information on the page is necessarily encrypted or secured. The last option in the **Security** section of the Chrome **Options** window (refer to Figure 6.1) involves how you should display such information in a website, as shown in Figure 6.2. You can choose whether to display all content regardless of whether it is secure, you can choose to display insecure images, or you can block all insecure content.

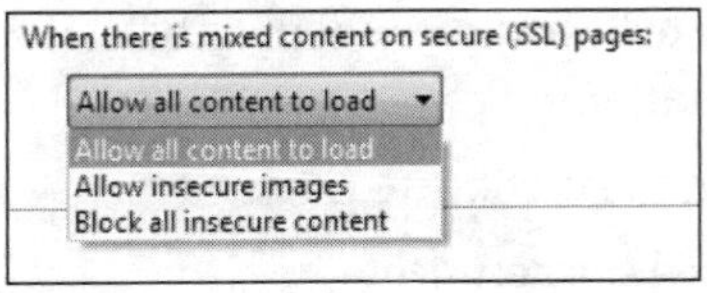

FIGURE 6.2

Some secure pages display insecure content; Chrome lets you decide how to handle mixed content.

The most technically advanced option on the Under the Hood tab, the Manage Certificates button, is also the one we saved for last. This option lets you manage trusted SSL certificates through the Certificates window as shown in Figure 6.3.

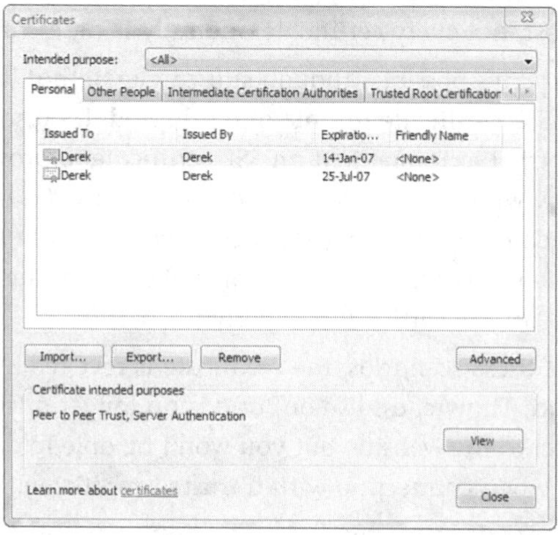

FIGURE 6.3

Chrome lets you manage your trusted certificates so you can visit secure websites with confidence.

The Certificates window is the central location for finding out all relevant information about the SSL certificates that communicate with Chrome. The list of trusted certificates is displayed by purpose (by default, all are displayed). From the **Intended Purpose** drop-down menu, you can sort the certificates by category; this could be **Client Authentication**, **Secure Email**, **Advanced Purposes**, or **All**.

The relevant trusted certificates appear below; each certificate displays the following information:

- To whom the certificate is issued
- Who issued the certificate
- The expiration date
- The friendly name

You can find out specific details about the purpose of the certificate by clicking it; specific details appear in the bottom portion of the Certificates window, as shown in Figure 6.4.

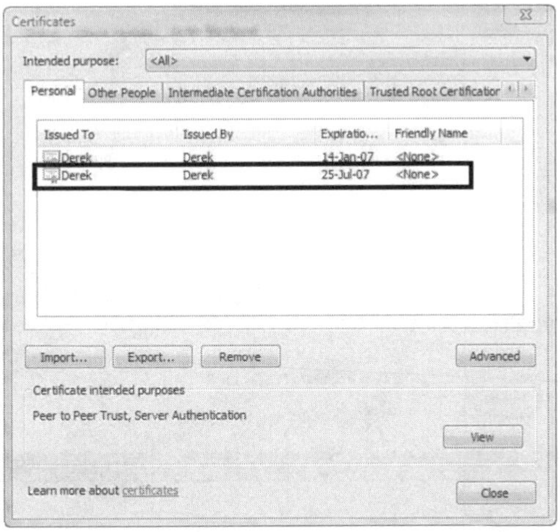

FIGURE 6.4

You can find out more about the purpose of a certificate by clicking it.

The Certificates window goes beyond the scope of the actual Chrome web browser. In fact, it displays information that is beyond the scope of this book and encroaches on advanced Windows security territory.

It's important to remember that certificates are a serious business, and if you're not familiar with them and how they work, you're better off not manipulating them in any way. If you need more information on trusted certificates, the Windows online help is a good place to start.

What Threat Level?

Despite the anecdotal evidence indicating that online threats are a legitimate menace, it's a safe bet that most people don't really take them seriously. In fact, it's likely that your average home user doesn't take any additional steps to maintain online protection beyond the installation of an antivirus program and keeping the Windows Firewall enabled. In a way, Microsoft recognized this by including Windows Defender, which protects against malicious and unwanted software, in later versions of its Windows operating system (see Figure 6.5).

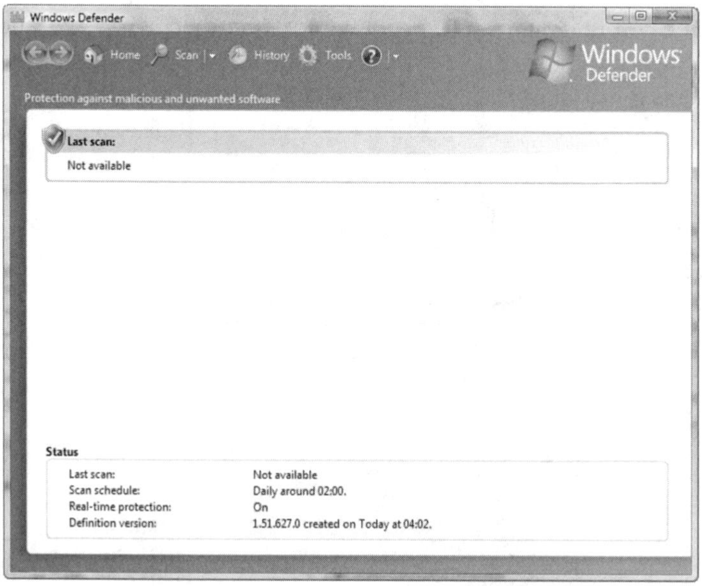

FIGURE 6.5

Windows Defender helps you reduce your computer's threat level.

However, it's important to take online threats seriously. In the past few chapters, you've read a lot about the various kinds of threats and quite a bit of jargon related to online threats. In the interest of helping you fully understand what these threats are, and how to deal with them, let's meet some of the major players.

Viruses

For starters, there's the classic virus threat. The oldie, but goodie, of online threats, the computer virus is often sent as a file attachment in an email or disguised as a file download. When downloading files (especially multimedia or zip files), it is crucial that you scan the files using antivirus software before opening or unzipping the files on your machine.

Some developers are either not too bright, or don't think very highly of computer users, so they either forget or don't bother to hide the extension of their file. One such giveaway is when the file appears to have multiple extensions, like the (in)famous .scr or .bat extension, often followed by a more familiar extension such as .doc or .zip.

Viruses can wreak a lot of havoc, but it's also important to be aware of hoaxes. Some websites, such as snopes.com, are dedicated to killing rumors and stopping the spread of false information with regard to computer viruses.

A good example of a hoax that you may have seen is the email that circulates that claims that the plastic in water bottles is deadly if it's reused or frozen. The email is pretty convincing, and it's enough to scare you right out of drinking bottled water...only it's not true. In fact, snopes.com debunks the hoax at: http://www.snopes.com/medical/toxins/petbottles.asp.

That's not to say that real threats do not exist; to find out more about what viruses are and what they can do, Microsoft provides an informative website on the topic at http://www.microsoft.com/protect/computer/basics/virus.mspx.

The best way to manage computer viruses is to use antivirus software in conjunction with your web browser. Neither Windows nor Chrome provides built-in antivirus protection, so it's up to you to make sure that there is one to protect your entire system.

Spyware

The next threat that you need to understand is the concept of spyware. When you visit websites, the host website can plant little pieces of software called spyware on your computer through your web browser. In more innocuous, yet still annoying, cases, this software may report on your surfing habits and report back to the host website for later use in a sort of guerrilla marketing tactic.

However, spyware can be much more dangerous than that. For example, more ill-intended spyware can do things such as slow down your computer system by consuming system resources, modify your web browser's home page, and otherwise invade your privacy.

Some antivirus software packages can also manage spyware; however, a number of free software packages are dedicated to the surveillance and removal of spyware software. These applications, like antivirus software, should be regularly updated to make sure that your computer keeps up with spyware technology.

Trojans

Another important threat is the Trojan horse. The Trojan horse is a piece of malware that seems innocent enough at first but quickly takes a turn for the worse. In many cases, a Trojan horse takes control of your computer and seemingly starts by doing the right thing. Once it has gained access to your system, a Trojan starts doing its own thing, and the results are rarely favorable.

For example, a Trojan can unleash a flurry of scripts designed to systematically take down your computer faster than the Greeks took control of Troy in Greek mythology. Often, if the Trojan (or worm) has spread sufficiently, there's nothing left to do but completely wipe your hard drive and start anew.

All these threats are avoidable, but they could still happen to any one of us. Other online threats simply require you to exercise some common sense and not fall prey to them.

A Phishing Reminder

Earlier in the book, you may recall the discussion of phishing. Everyone at some point will receive an email pretending to be, for example, from customer support for your bank. The email often asks you to confirm personal information via a link that is in the email. The link in the email points, usually, to a different website that logs your personal data. By the way, that website would not be the site of the bank. This technique is also employed to obtain people's credit card details.

Chrome, as mentioned earlier in this chapter, does have a security feature that protects you against phishing. Your email client and/or antivirus software may also have a security feature that analyzes incoming email for phishing attempts.

These are hardly the only threats that stalk the Web. These are only the threats that you are most likely to encounter as you go online. Unfortunately, the creators of these threats are increasingly clever and are coming up with new and "better" viruses and threats. It's important that you regularly update your virus and malware detecting software.

Got Sand? Sandboxing Slows Attacks

Telling people not to work with distrusted sites or resources is wishful thinking. After all, some of us like to take risks, and others need to take risks in our line of work. In those situations, how can you do what needs to be done and still work within the same framework for your computer?

If you are technically inclined, you may want to consider a security technique called sandboxing. If you're familiar with software development, you may have heard of something called a *sandbox*, which is a controlled environment where developers and testers can try an "unsafe" product in a safe environment.

 A *sandbox* is a controlled environment that developers use to run untested code. The idea of the sandbox is to allow processes and applications to be isolated so they cannot alter other processes and applications until they've been tested.

Sandboxing is a similar concept, where a contained execution environment exists that allows testing unknown or potentially untrustworthy sites or applications. Since this type of environment limits the amount of access to files and resources, it slows down the spread of any potential threats, such as viruses or malware.

Sandboxing is a little different from a sandbox, but only in execution. The whole concept of sandboxing is built on the sandbox that developers use, but sandboxing takes place in your browser. It's an area that's used specifically for untested (or unproven) code executions as a method of protecting your computer from malicious software.

To put sandboxing in simple terms, it's really just cordoning off a section of your hard drive, as illustrated in Figure 6.6, and making it impenetrable to the rest of your hard drive (much like a virtual drive if you have ever used VMWare or Microsoft Virtual PC).

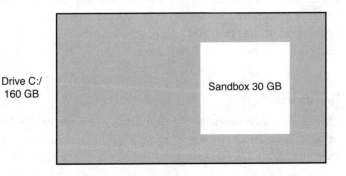

FIGURE 6.6

Sandboxing is one way of keeping unwelcome guests from crashing your computer.

Any applications that are installed or accessed from the sandbox stay completely within the sandbox. For example, if you were to download a file from

Chrome to the sandbox, and it just so happened to be a virus or spyware, the damage would be limited to the confines of the sandbox. Under no circumstances would the offending file be able to penetrate the borders of the sandbox and contaminate the rest of your system's memory.

This is a fine option for those who need to surf less-than-secure websites but still want to do so securely. Admittedly, it's not the most convenient option. There aren't any technological disadvantages to this solution, but do keep in mind that you do have to run a mini-environment that is parallel to your machine.

In other words, you need to make sure that you install Chrome in the sandbox to visit websites safely within your sandbox. If you fail to do so, you may find yourself on the receiving end of some unpleasant surprises—notably spyware, among others!

Your first reaction may be to wonder how to go about setting up a sandbox, or what you need to put up such a security system. Fortunately, in the 21st century world of personal computing, you no longer have to do it yourself.

A number of third-party solutions are available online that allow you to set up an out-of-the-box sandbox with little effort. If sandboxing seems like a viable option for you, think about a third-party solution to get yourself going.

As alluded to earlier in this section, another option is to use VMWare or Microsoft Virtual PC to create a separate, safe quarter on your computer. Like a sandbox, a virtual disk drive creates a virtual drive on your computer that is airtight.

If you installed Chrome on this virtual drive and inadvertently downloaded a virus, only data and resources on the virtual drive would be at risk. While this option is available (for free), the downside is that you must also install the operating system on the virtual drive.

Closing the Door

This introduction to online threats names just a few of the threats that you might encounter as you use Chrome. Fortunately, they are all manageable using the available preventive software and technologies.

A number of attractive options were provided throughout the course of this chapter that would allow you to securely work with distrusted websites or potentially dangerous online content.

Tinkering Around Under the Hood

In this part:

- An Open Source Overview
- Developing Sites for Chrome
- Spit-Shining Chrome
- Make It Yours

Part of what makes Google Chrome so different from other browsers is that it's based on open source code, so you can monkey around with it to truly make Chrome your own web browser.

In this part of the book, you learn a bit more about the customization that you can add to Chrome if you're willing to play with the code. Of course, there's a preface that tells you a bit more about why and how all the parts of Chrome work so that you don't really make any mistakes while you're following the examples in the book.

When you're finished with this part, though, you should feel pretty comfortable tinkering around with Chrome. And who knows, maybe your friends will be amazed at the cool things you've done with your browser.

Open Source Overview

Imagine that you could offer input on the features included in the business software you purchase. Imagine that you could actually define the features you need, find the basic software package you like, and request your custom features to be added, instead of having to make due with software that does almost, but not quite, everything you need, or whose interface you dislike or is difficult to use.

Now, imagine you could have this flexibility and customization for a fraction of the cost of standard proprietary software packages. Sounds like a dream world, doesn't it?

Believe it or not, the ability to design and customize your own business software is not a dream. It's called open source, and it's the building block behind the Internet and Google Chrome.

Everyone Can Participate

Open source evolved from a simple spirit of cooperation and collaboration into a worldwide community of like-minded developers and users.

The concept of open source is to develop quality software and share the *source code* so that other developers can use your code to improve and build on the application. As software developers add to or change code to meet the needs of their clients, the software becomes better, more complete, and better able to meet the needs of those who use it. At the same time, people become better programmers because they can examine, learn from, and build on the code of those who have gone before them. With open source, there is no need to reinvent the wheel, so developers can spend more time solving the problem at hand and less time re-creating the basics.

geek speak   *Source code* is the instructions that tell the computer what to do. It's written in programming languages such as C++ or Visual Basic and translated into something the computer can understand using a separate program, called a compiler. It is the source code that falls under the various software license types.

The resulting software is released to the public under an open source or free software license. There are several types of open licenses. Most provide the user with the right to examine and change source code without the need to further compensate the originating developer. In most cases, you also have the right to redistribute the software with your changes as long as you don't charge for the software. For example, if you download the source code for Chromium and add functionality, you may freely distribute your software package, but you may not charge users, and you also must release your software under the open source license. Many open source licenses also give users the right to distribute the original software, exactly as they acquired it.

geek speak   Chromium is the project behind Google Chrome web browser. Google uses the Chromium project code as the base code for Chrome. Then, the Chrome team adds elements that make it uniquely theirs to create Google Chrome. You will find Chromium at the website, here: http://code.google.com/chromium/.

7

WHAT IS A SOFTWARE LICENSE?

A *software license* is an agreement between you, the end user, and the software company that outlines the responsibilities and rights of each party. This is the long bit of text you must agree to in order to install new software on your computer. It is also called the EULA, or End User License Agreement. There are many different forms of software licenses. Some proprietary EULAs specify that the user cannot install the software on more than one machine. Others may specify that content created may be used only for specific purposes, or that you agree to allow spyware to be installed on your computer along with the software. Most open source licensing agreements specify how and under what conditions the user may access, change, and redistribute the source code. That's why it's important to always read the fine print before installing any software on your computer or using online applications.

Many people see open source licensing as a new idea in software development, but in truth this was the original development model.

In the early 1960s many computers came with free license software. This software could be shared among users, and the source code was open and available to look at, learn from, and improve on for anyone who was interested. Other developers were encouraged to dig into the code to modify and improve the application. The belief was this would not only create better software but better developers, as well. This was the beginning of telecommunications protocols and ultimately led to the creation of the Internet.

Then, in the late 1960s IBM had a change of heart and decided to start licensing software to restrict distribution by users and forbid community programmers from examining the source code. Enter the first proprietary software. This evolved into the closed licenses we're all familiar with—software that the end user is not allowed to distribute, cannot access the source code, and most definitely may not modify in any way. Many proprietary licenses even ban you from installing the software on more than one machine. You must purchase a separate copy for each computer you own.

Even though proprietary software became the norm, the open source license didn't die. It just took the scenic route to the mainstream. Hundreds of open source programs are available for nearly every task you can imagine. Whether you want to run a complicated robot or simply track your household budget, you have many open source programs to choose from. The most commonly known open source applications are used to run the Internet.

Most people don't realize it, but most of the Internet is powered by open source software. From the servers that host the websites you depend on, to the applications used to access databases, open source runs the Web.

One of the most popular web server setups is known as the LAMP server. LAMP stands for Linux, Apache, MySQL, and Programming languages.

Linux is the operating system that runs the server computer and is responsible for making sure all the individual parts, both hardware and software, can talk to each other effectively. The operating system is what allows the system administrator to talk to the computer.

Apache is responsible for interpreting and fulfilling requests from users. This is done through HTML and web browsers, such as Google Chrome. Apache lets you access web pages, log in to your account, access your bank or online shopping accounts through secure servers (SSL), and allows you to use dynamic web content. Apache is also responsible for giving you those annoying error messages when your favorite website is down.

MySQL talks to any databases on the server, so users can access and manipulate information from their browsers. If you've ever accessed your bank information, used a public calendar, or viewed an online catalog, MySQL was probably working behind the scenes to give you the information you needed.

Programming languages, such as PHP, Python, Perl, and the latest, Ruby On Rails, give the server the ability to understand and respond to user requests. When the user does something—clicks the Pay Now button, for example— these languages run the script that submits your credit card information and submits your invoice and purchase order so the people responsible for filling your order know what you've ordered and where to send it.

These open source programs work together with your web browser to provide seamless access to the vast network of computers we call the Internet. They are essential to the smooth operation of the Internet as we know it. And, while they were developed with very different functions in mind and written in different programming languages, the one thing they have in common is that they are released under the open source license. Proprietary applications are available that do the same thing as the LAMP applications. Most of them are just as good as any of the applications in the LAMP model, but the open source license gives the user more flexibility, more up-to-date software, and a community of dedicated programmers who are responsive to the user's needs.

Table 7.1 outlines some major differences between open source and proprietary licenses. Let's take a closer look at how a couple of these differences affect both the home and medium-sized business user.

Cost

When you purchase a proprietary license for your home computer, most times you are legally required to pay for each copy of the software you use. If you want to install the software on each of the three PCs in your home, you are required to purchase three separate copies of the software. This gives you license to install and use the software on three machines. There are variations on proprietary licenses that allow you to install the software on any system you own for strictly personal use. Always read the license that accompanies software you purchase.

Business users purchase their proprietary licenses in bundles of 20, 50, 100, or more. If you have 20 machines with licensed software installed and your business adds another 16 machines, you have to pay for a 20 license bundle. You may save the additional four licenses until you need them. But, what happens if you upgrade your systems before you add those four machines? You're out the cost of the four licenses for your old machines and have to purchase the upgrade licenses as well.

In comparison, most open source software is free for the home user. A few open source applications charge a small fee for their use. In addition, some open source distributors charge for a business or mass use license, but many do not. Software updates are almost always included for free.

Turnaround time for bug fixes and software improvements

If you're using proprietary software, you don't have a lot of say in the development and improvement process. Fixes and updates are dictated by the company and released when the company feels these updates are needed. Usually, things like security and major bugs are fixed in a matter of a month or two. But for major improvements and feature upgrades, you may wait for a year or more. When the new software is finally released, there is no guarantee the upgrade request you asked for was included in the new version.

7

Table 7.1   Differences Between Open Source and Proprietary Licenses

Open Source	Proprietary
Usually (but not always) free to use.	Fee based on number of computers on which you plan to install the software.
Updated regularly, some with nightly builds.	Must wait for next release to upgrade. Many times you must pay for an upgrade license.
Community-based means you report program bugs directly to the developer team via email or bug tracker programs.	You must call tech support and go through channels to report bugs.
Bugs are fixed quickly and patches released with next update. Sometimes this happens overnight, and other or times it takes a week or two.	Patches and security fixes are released and sent to registered users for free. Sometimes it takes weeks months for patches to be released.
You can submit suggestions for improvements directly to the development team. Most developers are responsive to user requests. They like hearing from you.	You can submit suggestions for improvements, but developers have to answer to the company. Your suggestions are less likely to be implemented.
Add-ons and additional functionality may be developed and released by other than the original development team. Many programs have hundreds of add-ons to choose from and they are relatively easy to find.	Community add-ons may be available, but they can be difficult to find, and programs that allow them are few and far between.
You, or anyone, may look at the source code. You can make changes to meet your own needs.	You may not, under any circumstances, view the source code. Code is considered a trade secret. You agree to this when you install the software.
There is no paid service agreement or tech support, but there are many online forums where you can ask experienced users for help.	You pay for (sometimes limited) tech support when you purchase your license.
Most open source applications have online manuals and wiki pages.	You receive a user's manual that tells you how to install and run the software.
Customize the user interface to meet your needs and preferences. You can do this through add-ons. Or, if you're the programming type, by tweaking the source code to meet your needs.	You use the application as it was developed. No customization allowed, unless you can find add-ons for the application.
Most open source programs are designed to be cross-compatible and read file types formed by the various competing applications.	Most proprietary software expects you to use only their software, so they don't usually read other formats.

7

Open source works differently. Most open source developers maintain a bug fix page and discussion forum. This is where you, the user, get to contribute to the development process. Let's say that while using the software you find a feature that is missing. You go to the forum page listed in the online documentation and file a bug report. Usually, someone on the development team emails you for clarification of the problem. Once he understands the issue you're having or the feature you need, he forwards this information to the appropriate person or team. Often, you can opt to be included in this email. The responsible person either fixes the bug or designs a patch to provide the function you requested, and an updated release is sent out. Or the person emails those involved to explain why it can't or shouldn't be done. Either way you, the user with the issue, are kept fully informed of what is going on with your bug report. You can always opt out of this process if you don't have the time or inclination to be involved. This entire process usually happens in a matter of weeks, instead of the months we've come to expect from proprietary software.

For the home or business user, this means an opportunity to participate in the planning and developing stage of software development. It also means a direct, or fairly direct, line to the people creating the software, and the ability to change the software to meet individual needs. In the end, it means better, more flexible software for less money.

It Takes a Village: Open Source Is Collaboration

There are several steps to software development. Each step is important to the overall quality of the resulting software. Without open source, the time from ideation to completed project can take several months.

In the world of proprietary software the process looks like this: First, the idea needs to be formed and fleshed out. Ideation usually occurs to solve a problem or improve on a current software solution. Someone says, "Hey, wouldn't it be great if we had a program that let our customers purchase our widgets online?" The person who needs the application might outline the key functions of the program. He might run the idea by his business partner, and the two of them work together to list every function they want the program to have.

Next, these businessmen hire an outside application developer to develop and write the program. The developer researches existing applications that fulfill

7

the same or similar functions. She takes notes on functions existing programs have and what additional functionality is needed. She lays out a preliminary application plan and goes back to research a bit more. At this point, she compares the needs of the client with the programming languages at her disposal and chooses the platform that best meets the needs of both the application and the client. Then, she sits down and creates the application by writing and compiling the code.

After the software developer is finished, she passes the new application to the software tester. It's the tester's job to put the program through its paces, to make sure it does everything the developer claims, and to find programming bugs or errors. Many software testers or quality control people joke that their job is to break what the developer worked so hard to create. And in many ways that's true. You want your software tester to find any problems so the developer can fix them before the application gets to the end user.

WHERE DOES BETA TESTING FIT IN?

There are several basic differences between the beta testing that happens on the Web and the private testing we're talking about here. Beta testing amounts to the application being released to the end user with the understanding that the user may find an error or two or that features are still being added. Under beta testing, the user is expected to contact the development team through bug reporting websites, email, or another prearranged method in the event the user encounters a problem with the software or wants to request a feature be added. This method allows the end user to have input in the final development of the application. Google Chrome came out of beta testing in December 2008. Another familiar Google application, Gmail, is still in beta testing.

When the tester is finished, he sends his notes on what is broken and what should be improved back to the developer. The developer completes the fixes and sends the improved application back to the tester. This continues until the tester clears the application as complete.

Finally, after several months of waiting, the end user gets the customized software he paid for.

In the open source world this process is significantly shorter.

The ideation stage is the same. Someone needs a custom function from a program. He makes a list of the new functions he needs from his current application. The user hands this spec sheet off to the developer, along with an open source copy of the application he is currently using.

The developer opens the source code and examines it. Then she researches to see whether the improvements she's making have been done before.

If it has, she copies the code, tweaks it to meet the specific needs of her client, and inserts the new code into the source code of the original application. Usually, at this point she shares her new code with other open source programmers by including it in the libraries and lists.

If there is no code out there, she writes only the code that provides the functionality her client needs. This new code is added to the original code.

The application is then tested, perfected, and sent to the end user just like the proprietary model.

The key difference here is that in the open source model the improved software may be released in its entirety for others to use. Or the additional code might be released as an add-on so that other users can add this new code to their existing application and extend the functionality of their programs as well.

Other users and programmers throughout the open source world continue this process. Each programmer improves and adds code to the project. Eventually, you have an application with hundreds of add-ons and extended usability that the original developer could have never achieved on his own.

This collaboration between users and programmers all over the world leads to a more complete ideation process, creative sharing, and better constructed applications. In addition, this model encourages developers to work together and learn from each other.

This idea of collaboration making better programs and better developers is what fuels the open source market.

Putting the Chromium in Chrome

Google Chrome is a shining star for the open source method of designing, writing, and building software. A group of developers at Google were talking about the future of the Web and comparing their favorite browsers. They came to the conclusion that even the best browser on the Web wasn't equipped to handle the way Internet usage is developing.

7

Internet programs, or web applications, are becoming a popular way for web users to handle their daily business. Whether it's personal, school, or work, people all over the world are turning to web applications for word processing, communication, and managing business and household finances. Even tasks like project management, scheduling, and international meetings are being done via the Internet.

The Google developers realized there wasn't one single browser on the Web that was able to fully maximize today's technology. They decided to build a browser better able to handle these complex tasks, by combining the best browser features on the Web into one browser. The Chromium open source web browser was born.

Then, the same Google developers added specialized security features such as real-time malware and phishing protection, user stats and crash reporting, and *RLZ parameter* reporting to create Google Chrome.

geek speak

The *RLZ parameter* is made of encoded information about your version of Google Chrome. It includes information like from where you downloaded Chrome, when you installed it, and when you first used specific Chrome features. This information is sent to Google whenever you use Chrome's built-in search bar to perform a search. Google assures users this information is completely anonymous and is only used to evaluate whether specific groups of people are using Chrome.

⚡ At this point, you may be wondering what exactly is the difference between the open source Chromium and Google Chrome?

That's a great question, and the short answer is not much.

⚡ Chromium is the open source package. Developers can go to the Web and download the source code for Chromium. Then those developers can modify the code to change or enhance the functionality. Google fully supports this and even gives directions for downloading source code, sending in bug fixes, and submitting your code for possible inclusion in the official release. You find more information on how to do this on the Chromium website, at http://code.google.com/chromium/.

⚡ Chrome, on the other hand, is Google's official version release of Chromium. It includes the features that allow it to talk to Google servers to give you specialized functions such as malware and phishing protection. Chrome is also open source.

It's possible that in time the Chromium project and the Chrome web browser may evolve in different directions to become very different applications. As the open source community builds on Chromium, it will meet the needs of various types of web users. Likewise, Google Chrome will evolve as Google's vision of the Web changes.

Ultimately, to understand how Google Chrome works, you first need to understand Chromium.

Kits

Google Chrome developers started with an open source web toolkit. To put it simply, a web toolkit, or engine, is a small application that tells your computer how to interpret HTML and JavaScript. This interpretation dictates how your computer draws or renders web pages on your screen. Several of these toolkits are available, and after consulting with the Google Android team, the Chrome team decided to use WebKit. They downloaded the source code for WebKit and built Chromium by adding, removing, and changing components as needed.

> **Yellow Box** You can download WebKit yourself from http://webkit.org/.
> You find everything you need to participate in the WebKit project on this website.

Although this may seem like taking shortcuts, you need to remember this is the way open source software works. Web toolkits are small but involved pieces of programming. They take months to create and really are living, breathing programs themselves. The developers of WebKit are constantly adjusting, adapting, and improving to meet *W3C* standards and improve *Acid testing* scores. In fact, WebKit provides daily updates, called nightly builds, for developers and testers who choose to use them. While nightly builds are not intended for the general, everyday user, they are a vital piece of the puzzle for hard-core developers and web testers.

W3C stands for World Wide Web Consortium. This organization is made up of member organizations from around the world. Members work together to establish and maintain programming standards for the Internet. To learn more about the W3C, what they do, or how to become a member check out the official website, http://www.w3.org/.

Acid tests are a series of tests designed to challenge the way a given web browser translates and renders HTML and XML. Acid tests also test the JavaScript capabilities of the browser. You can find out exactly what is involved in Acid testing, and even run Acid tests on your web browsers at the Web Standards Project Acid Tests website, http://www.acidtests.org/.

When developers strive to meet or exceed W3C standards and improve Acid test scores, users get a faster, more powerful browser that can properly display and navigate any website and run any web application.

Using WebKit meant the Chromium team could spend more time and resources developing the interface, features, and security that make a web browser great.

And that's exactly what they did. The web browser developers at Google took the best parts of other browsers and incorporated those features into Chromium. Some of these features had open source code available, which had to be changed and adjusted to fit into the WebKit platform, and others needed to be coded from scratch.

The part of the browser the user sees and interacts with is called the *user interface* (UI). This includes tabs, buttons, toolbars, and the display area. The UI must interpret the information coming at it from both the Web and the user. This is accomplished by a collection of programming pieces. These pieces work together with the WebKit to create a working browser.

The piece closest to WebKit is called the WebKit Core. This plugs directly into WebKit and provides translation between WebKit and the computer's operating system.

Next is what Google calls WebKit Glue. This section of the code translates from "Googlespeak code" into "WebKit speak."

Imagine it this way. You have a small ball. This ball needs to run a huge machine. It knows how to do many things but only speaks Latin. That's WebKit.

Place a second ball around the first. This second ball translates instructions from Latin to Greek and Japanese. It performs this task flawlessly, but that's all it can do. That's WebKit Port.

Now, put a third ball around the second. This ball translates all the languages from the outside world into either Greek or Latin. That's WebKit Glue.

Everything else connects into these balls. Figure 7.1 shows a diagram of how this works. Keep in mind, of course, we're talking about computer programs and not any type of physical object.

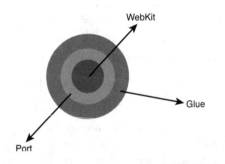

FIGURE 7.1
While it's not a true model, this diagram gives you an idea of how the WebKit, WebKit Port, and WebKit Glue fit together to give you flawless communication between computer processor and Internet.

Threads

As you dig into the code that makes up Chromium, you'll notice quite a few separate programming threads. The concept of threads is important. Threads act as dedicated pathways to and from the WebKit. Think of threads as highways designated to get certain types of information to the main distributer as quickly as possible, or store information in the most secure manner possible. Here is an overview of some of the threads Chromium uses:

- **UI thread**—The main pathway. Each command the user issues via mouse or keyboard and each script or direction given by the server must travel through the UI thread.

- **file_thread**—Talks to the programs that let you save files to a hard drive or removable media, complete an Internet file transfer, or start your chat program. The file_thread talks to programs and processes on your hard drive and gives them instructions.

- **db_thread**—Handles most database requests. Most applications use databases to organize and store information. Chromium uses special programs to talk to these databases. The db_thread is where this communication happens.

- **io_thread**—Where communication between the processes happens. When the render process needs to find out what the browser process is doing, this is where it happens. If a tab needs to ask the main system for more memory, for example, it uses the io_thread.

- **Web data**—Stores Internet-related tidbits of information such as your passwords and most frequently used keywords. Storage in a dedicated thread means your passwords are recalled faster and adds an extra layer of protection in case of a malware attack.

- **History**—Saves information related to your web browsing history.

- **safe_browsing**—Where the phishing and malware list information is stored and updated.

Have you ever been frustrated by a browser that seems to slow to a crawl every time you try to do something? Browsers hang up when the pathway to or from the web engine gets clogged with information. By creating these separate pathways, Chromium reduces browser hanging and increases your online security. Figure 7.2 adds threads to our WebKit diagram.

Processes

The next component of the Chromium browser is the process. A process is a group of code that performs a specialized function. Continuing with our model, each process is like a self-contained box. Data becomes part of the process because it travels on the threads that go through that process.

The Browser process is responsible for managing most of the threads. Think of it like a box that the majority of threads run through. The Browser process acts as a manager and traffic cop to coordinate and make sure everything runs smoothly. This is the main process that runs the overall web browser.

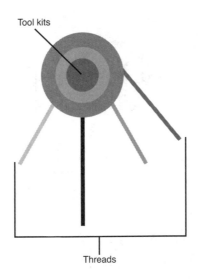

Tool kits

Threads

FIGURE 7.2

Threads keep the flow of information moving. Each line in this diagram represents a different thread.

The Render process represents each window or tab the user has open. This process communicates with the WebKit to interpret HTML and put the page on the screen. There is a separate Render process for each tab or window the user opens, and every Render process has its own separate line to the WebKit. Figure 7.3 adds the final building block to our diagram.

Sandboxing helps keep your computer safe from malware by restricting the communication between all these components. By requiring tabs and windows to maintain separate Render processes and making all communications go through the Browser process, system resources are protected. In addition, every Render process occurs on its own layer, much like stacked sheets of paper to prevent one corrupted Render process from affecting another, uncorrupted process.

geek speak   *Sandboxing* is a programming term that means to completely separate a program from the rest of the system. The sandboxed program has its own memory and can't talk to any other program on the computer, much like a child playing alone in her own sandbox.

7

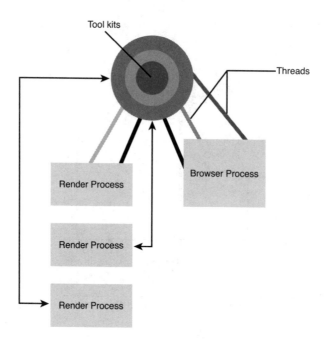

FIGURE 7.3

Processes add an extra level of security to the browsing experience.

This whole thing is called multiprocess resource loading, and it's the backbone of Chromium. This is one of the main things that makes Chromium different from the majority of available browsers.

Libraries and Scripts

We're almost done, but there are few other components you need to understand before you can start optimizing your websites for Chrome.

In addition to these processes and threads are libraries and scripts that add functions. These are called *back-end functions*.

geek speak *Back-end functions* are small programs embedded or plugged into larger applications. These smaller programs provide added capabilities.

Skia is an open source code graphic engine that adds rendering and graphic functionality to Chrome. Skia helps determine how and how quickly screen images appear. Skia is written in C++ and is smaller than some of the other graphic engines. A few specific functions include

- Speeds up the onscreen drawing of texture and shading
- Translates image files such as JPG, PNG, BMP, and others
- Interprets certain types of animations

If you're working on the Web, you absolutely need to interpret and run JavaScript. That's where the open source V8 comes in. Developed by Google, V8 JavaScript engine is compatible with Windows XP, Windows Vista, Mac OS X 10.5, and most *Linux distros*. V8 is written in C++.

geek speak

Linux distros, or distributions, are open source operating systems based on the Linux kernel. Many distros are available to Linux users, and each provides a unique user experience. Red Hat, Debian, and Ubuntu are examples of popular Linux distros. They are the open source equivalent to Windows XP, Windows Vista, Mac OS, and others.

LEAN MORE ABOUT OPEN SOURCE BACK-END PROGRAMS

BuildBot—http://buildbot.net/trac

Skia—http://gigaom.com/2008/09/02/google-open-sources-skia-graphics-engine/

S Cons—http://www.scons.org/

V8—http://code.google.com/p/v8/

Ensuring a Flawless Application

When you're constantly updating, changing, and improving the pieces that make up a large application, you also need to continually test those updates to be sure they work like they're supposed to. For this vital job, Chromium uses a program called BuildBot. This open source program automatically detects changes in the application code and runs tests to ensure flawless performance. If an error is found, the program flags it and notifies the developer who made the changes.

7

And to bring all these pieces together and make them into one seamlessly running application is the open source tool SCons. Written in the Python programming language, SCons takes all the individual components and reduces them to the only language any processor can understand, machine language.

What does all this mean for you? For the nontechnical, you get a top rate, secure, easy-to-use browser that is fast and flexible enough to handle today's most demanding use. The open source nature of both Chromium and Chrome means you get faster updates, so the browser can keep up with the needs of tomorrow, as well.

For the technogeeks among us, Google has given you a great browser to play in, and all the documentation you need to build add-ons, expand functionality, and show off your programming skills.

Closing the Door

So now you have a thorough understanding of the open source philosophy and how that works in practice. We talked about the pieces of a LAMP server and how they work together with your browser to give you the best Internet experience possible. You also know how all the pieces of Chrome fit together to make the browser. In the next chapter, we talk about developing or optimizing your website to look and respond its best in Chrome.

Developing Sites for Chrome

Many web browsers are available today. Many of them are even open source. A few of them are good, solid browsers with a lot of features and quick rendering times. They all support JavaScript, Flash, and most other features found on the Web. So, what makes Google Chrome different from the rest?

The difference is in the individual parts of Chrome, which include WebKit, V8, and Gears. WebKit is a first-class rendering engine that lends itself nicely to accepting gadgets and making life easy for developers. V8 compiles, interprets, and runs JavaScript in record time. It's the fastest JavaScript engine available right now. And, Gears adds a level of portability to web applications that was never possible before.

The flexibility of WebKit, speed of V8, and portability of Gears work together to create a top of the line web browser that keeps up with the way we use the Internet today. When you understand what each component does, and how they work together, you can begin develop websites and web applications that take full advantage of what Google Chrome has to offer.

8

Is This Part of the WebKit?

Every computer needs a system to interpret data, turn it into graphics and display those graphics on your screen so you can view it. This process is completed by a computer program, called a rendering, or layout, engine. When you visit a website or use a web application, the image you see on the monitor is transmitted via the Internet to your computer. The information comes in the form of HTML, XML, image, CSS, and XSL files.

As part of your web browser, the layout engine reads these files, and then displays them on your monitor, pixel by pixel. It's a bit like painting a picture, but it happens so quickly that we usually perceive it as an instantaneous event.

Each web browser development team chooses the layout engine they feel best meets the needs of the browser they are creating. Development teams evaluate functions such as rendering speed, ability to accept plug-ins and expansions, license restrictions, operating system compatibility, and performance on Acid tests.

Every well known web browser uses a different layout engine. Differences in the way each layout engine is built affects how some web pages look on your screen. Have you every viewed a web page on your home computer, and then viewed the same page in a different web browser on your work computer? If so, you may have noticed slight differences in how the page looked. These differences are most obvious when you're switching from Internet Explorer to most other browsers. That's because Internet Explorer uses a layout vastly different than any of the others. Table 8.1 shows each popular web browser, the layout engine it's based on, platform, and the latest Acid Test scores available at the time of this writing.

Table 8.1   How Do the Layout Engines Compare?

Web Browser(s)	Layout Engine	Platforms Supported	Acid Test Scores	License Type
Firefox	Gecko	Windows Linux Mac OS X	71/100	Open Source
Konqueror	KHTML	Windows Mac OS X Unix-like	85/100	Open Source
Opera	Presto	Windows Linux Mac OS X	85/100	Proprietary
Internet Explorer	Trident (also called MSHTML)	Windows	20/100	Proprietary

Web Browser(s)	Layout Engine	Platforms Supported	Acid Test Scores	License Type
Chrome	WebKit	Windows	79/100	Open Source
Safari		Mac Linux	75/100	

As you can see from the table, Presto and KHTML perform a little better on Acid Test 3 than does WebKit. So, why did the Chrome team choose WebKit? Ultimately, they needed a layout engine that was small, because running a multiprocess browser requires many instances of the layout engine to be open at one time. In addition, the layout engine they chose couldn't have a lot of extra features attached to it, or it would interfere with sandboxing the browser. And, of course, since Chrome was to be an open source browser, the layout also had to be open source.

The Google Android team used WebKit as the basis for Google's mobile browser, and had nothing but great things to say about the flexibility, simplicity, and ease of use they found in WebKit. And so, they made the decision to go with WebKit when developing Chrome.

In perfect open source tradition, WebKit sprouted from earlier versions of the *KHTML* and *KJS* projects. Written in C++, WebKit works hard behind the scenes to interpret *MIME* types, *markup*, and other formatting information and display it on your screen. WebKit also is responsible for talking to http servers and interpreting your mouse clicks.

geek speak

KHTML is an HTML rendering engine developed by the same people who came up with the K desktop environment for Unix-like systems. The first version of KHTML was released in late 1998.

KJS was developed in 2000 as the JavaScript interpreter for KDE's Konqueror web browser.

MIME type is an overview term for the various ways data is put together in cyberspace. Some familiar MIME types include application/x-javascript, application/pdf, image/jpg application/zip, and audio/mpeg.

Markup is a system of noting how text should be displayed onscreen. Typically referred to as *markup languages*, these systems are not real computer languages, since they lack the required components to be considered a language. (By definition, a real programming language must contain tests, branches, and loops.) Some common examples of markup are HTML (HyperText Markup Language) and XML (eXtensible Markup Language).

WebKit was one of the first engines to pass the Acid 3 test. This speed fit in well with Google's goals for Chrome. The Google team wanted to provide users with the fastest, most stable, and most secure web browser on the Web. And they wanted it to handle the web applications of today, and in the future.

That speed and flexibility mean better-looking web pages and faster perform-ing web applications. Added stability lets users do more with your web appli-cations without worrying about a browser crash taking out everything they're working on at once. And extra security—Chrome automatically warns users when they are about to access a website that is known to contain malware or a phishing scheme—gives users peace of mind and makes them more likely to use web applications or online storage.

Chrome is the ideal web browser for people who rely on web applications to work remotely. The multiprocess architecture discussed in Chapter 7, "Open Source Overview," helps Chrome process multiple user requests quickly with-out crashing.

In addition, the streamlined and minimalist interface lets you do what you need to without being distracting or getting in the way.

One of Google's goals for Chrome was to create a browser that made it easy for developers to optimize toward. WebKit is one way they've done this. By developing a browser that operates from WebKit, and is intended to respond and render almost exactly like the popular Safari web browser, Chrome devel-opers took an important step toward streamlining web development with the goal of improving web content across all browsers and platforms. As web browsers become more consistent, users and developers will spend less time focusing on browser specifications and more time developing great content and web applications.

Several application projects now include Chrome in their optimization and supported browser list. You can even download a release of Chrome that is completely portable. It's called, simply enough, Google Chrome Portable. It runs from a memory stick. This allows users to run Chrome without installing it on the computer's hard drive. Since it runs from the memory stick, users are able to take their bookmarks, settings, passwords, and any other unique infor-mation stored within the browser with them. You can maintain your settings and continue your work on any computer with a USB port. Figure 8.1 shows Google Chrome Portable on a Windows Vista machine.

Even though add-ons and extensions aren't yet supported, plans to change that are in the works. In the meantime, though, users have the option of using *bookmarklets* to add the extension features they need. And with the slow but steady market share Chrome is gaining, it just makes good business sense to support and develop with Chrome in mind.

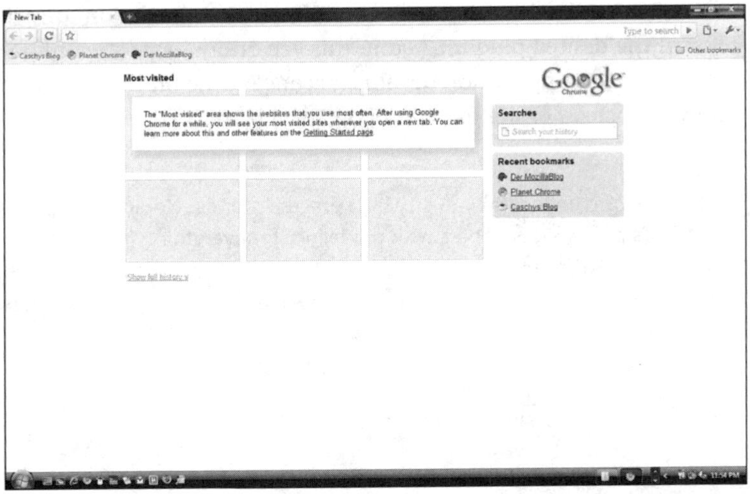

FIGURE 8.1
Chrome Portable looks and acts just like Google Chrome.

geek speak *Bookmarklets* are little chunks of code that allow you to expand the basic functionality of Google Chrome—everything from Stumble Upon features, a Twitter Client, digg, and even page translation.

Yellow Box

Google Chrome Portable includes all the best features of Chrome, but there's no need to install Chrome Portable. Just download, unpack, and run. Chrome Portable even saves your application shortcuts and import settings. It supports dynamic tabs and Incognito mode and includes the safer browsing access to malware and phishing lists. You can download it from http://www.chromeplugins.org/tips-tricks/latest-google-chrome-portable-usb-version/.

Another interesting plug-in for Chrome is Google Chrome Dual View. This one lets you split the display area down the middle and view two different websites in the same tab. You can find Dual View here: http://www.chromeplugins.org/plugins/google-chrome-dual-view/.

We talk more about this in Chapter 9, "Spit-Shining Chrome," but for now you can check them out for yourself at http://www.chromeplugins.org/google/.

Developing websites to look good and run quickly is easy. Really, all the web developer needs to do is follow *WC3 standards*. Since WebKit, and Chrome, readily accept all the popular plug-ins, there's nothing special the developer needs to do. As with other browsers, the user needs to manually download and install the desired plug-in. Again, this versatility helps streamline web development and lets application developers concentrate on the content they want to provide instead of the method of delivery.

geek speak   *WC3 standards* define the industry best practices for developing web pages. These standards provide developers with guidelines for everything from page accessibility for the disabled, to using XHTML on web pages. WC3 standards are not required, however most developers comply with the guidelines.

WHAT IS A PLUG-IN?

Plug-ins are small chunks of code that act as extensions to the basic browser. They allow the browser to interpret and execute specific kinds of code. The most common plug-ins (all supported by Google Chrome) are

- **Silverlight**—A video player for web and mobile devices, published by Microsoft (http://silverlight.net/).

- **Flash**—Adobe Flash Player enables your web browser to play animation created in Flash with Action Script (http://get.adobe.com/flashplayer/).

- **QuickTime**—Created by Apple, this movie player plays video created for many different platforms (http://www.apple.com/quicktime/).

- **Acrobat Reader**—Also from Adobe, Acrobat Reader enables your browser to read and display text in PDF format (http://www.adobe.com/products/reader/).

- **Real Player**—Another video player. Use it to play movies, listen to music, or play games in the form of Real Arcade (http://www.real.com/).

- **Java**—Developed by Sun Microsystems, Java is a programming language used to create web applications and online games. Users download and install a virtual machine to compile and run code within the web browser (http://java.com/en/).

- **Windows Media Player**—Used to play movies and listen to music (http://www.microsoft.com/windows/windowsmedia/default.mspx).

I Should've Had a V8

When I hear the phrase "V8," the first thing that comes to mind is juice; car engines run a close second. But that's about to change.

In today's Internet, JavaScript is the key to getting things done. JavaScript is a programming language that works from the user's computer to talk to the computer hosting the website. HTML is intended to provide users with layout and content. But, if you want to do anything with that content—process data on a form, for example—you need JavaScript. Additionally, the web browser uses JavaScript to control browser functions, like resizing or opening and closing windows. Web applications such as Google Docs and Gmail make extensive use of JavaScript.

Back in 2006, when Google was just starting on Chrome, the Google developers evaluated the available *JavaScript engines* and found them lacking. At the time JavaScript within the web browser had some issues. Top among the problems was speed. Executing JavaScript in any browser was painfully slow. The old Java engines bottlenecked and bogged down when faced with a large amount of code. They couldn't expand to meet object allocation needs, and users experienced *memory leaks* when using web applications.

geek speak

A *JavaScript engine* translates from JavaScript into machine language, so the computer processor can execute the code.

Despite the name, a *memory leak* has everything to do with how your system runs, and nothing to do with losing data. Every program borrows memory from the computer to run. When you close that program, it's supposed to give the borrowed memory back. If doesn't, that's called a memory leak. Typically, the missing memory stays unavailable until you reboot your system.

That's fine if all you're doing is surfing the Web, but the way we use the Web has changed a lot since 2006. There are fewer static web pages, more interactive content, and more people are using web apps such as online email, chat programs, and even online word processors. To flawlessly handle this kind of Internet usage, you need a JavaScript engine with some punch.

So, the Chrome team decided it was time to change the way JavaScript is handled within the browser. They envisioned a faster, more efficient JavaScript engine, and the only way to get that was to build a brand-new type of JavaScript engine from the bottom up.

They determined the best way to improve performance of the JavaScript engine was to completely change the way JavaScript was implemented. They analyzed JavaScript code and realized JavaScript could potentially be handled more efficiently if the engine categorized commands when the script was compiled, instead of at run time. The Google Team concluded this would best be done by using classes. Then they set out to develop a way to divide the dynamic JavaScript objects into classes. V8 does this through something called hidden classes.

You need a general understanding of JavaScript to understand how this works. Because JavaScript is a dynamic language objects and functions can be defined differently at various stages in the program. When JavaScript is compiled, the JavaScript engine must go through and sort out and define each *function*. Because of this, JavaScript can be slow to interpret, and slow to run.

geek speak   A *function* is a reusable block of code that tells the computer how to perform a specific task. Functions are called, or used, when the user clicks a link, opens a file, or otherwise gives a command for the computer to do something.

V8 looks at each function and defines it so that, for example, the function that defines a specific point is always in the same order, regardless of how the code is written. This is similar to the process of declaring and then defining variables in other programming languages.

If you are creating a set of points, V8 sets up a table in the background that states the format for the function "point" is (x, y), and then it lists the possible values for each component of that point.

When the program is run, V8 looks up functions and values in these hidden tables or classes. Google programmers found that about 90% of function classes are reused in every JavaScript application. Because of this, these hidden classes are saved and examined in relation to each JavaScript program you run. Instead of redefining functions separately for each program, V8 can simply look up the function to see whether it's already been defined. If it has, then V8 already knows how to execute the function. Then, based on the result of that lookup, the engine either executes the function or adds a new class to the library to define it.

While this may add a few extra seconds the first time a function is encountered, it definitely speeds up execution as that library is built.

Another way V8 helps speed up the overall function of Chrome is by utilizing inline caching. This is the process of calling and defining properties, so the computer learns to recognize each property and learns how to treat it. In V8, this is a four-step process that classifies each property based on the number of times it's been run. Each inline cache stub contains instructions on how to store the property being evaluated, based on how many times V8 has encountered that specific process.

Yellow Box
The first label of V8's inline caching protocol is Uninitialized. This means V8 has never seen that process before and tells the processor to always consult the hidden class library before executing the property.

The second time a property is encountered, it's marked as Premonomorphic. To run this property, the computer looks up and defines its hidden class and rewrites it to run instantly.

Monomorphic properties are those that V8 has encountered several times. The object class is included in code so it can run instantaneously. Obviously this is the fastest way to run properties or classes of JavaScript code, because it eliminates the need to look up the process.

If a property is classified as Megamorphic, it will always be looked up and won't replace its classification. This may be caused by a block of code that refers to a different hidden class than the library expects.

While this may seem like a lot of steps, building this library of processes ultimately makes JavaScript execute faster because it learns to recognize the most common processes and develops almost instant execution.

Yellow Box
Most applications are put through a two-step process to turn the development language into something the computer can understand.

First, the compiler translates from the development language into bytecode. This is a language understood by every processor, in every computer, anywhere on the planet.

When the program is run on its intended platform, the compiler hands off this unicode to the computer's processor, which translates to its specific machine code dialect.

In addition to the hidden classes and class transitions, V8 uses a one-pass code generator to quickly compile JavaScript directly to machine language. Instead of the usual two-step process, V8 translates directly to language both *X86* and *ARM instruction sets* can understand. Doing this increases the speed and accuracy of code execution, because it talks directly to the computer processor without the need for additional translation.

geek speak *X86 instruction set* refers to the dialect of machine language the computer processor understands. X86 processors run the majority of workstations and laptops in the world.

ARM instruction set refers to the machine language dialect of the processors in most mobile devices.

Memory leaks have been eliminated in V8 by efficient removal of no longer needed objects. By momentarily pausing execution of the program to gather and eliminate trash in cycles, V8 sidesteps the lag in performance experienced by other JavaScript engines at cleanup time. Pointers are updated with every garbage collection cycle, so V8 can keep track of every object and its pointer ensuring nothing is misidentified and memory is continuously reclaimed.

These basic changes in the way JavaScript is handled means V8 can handle large JavaScript applications quickly. Your web app runs faster, with fewer errors than in competing engines, giving you the opportunity to develop larger, more complex JavaScript applications than ever before. As our world becomes even more digitized, the need for large web applications continues to grow. In an attempt to cut costs businesses are encouraging employee flexibility by allowing workers to telecommute and are conducting important meetings and training sessions over the Internet. V8's innovative handling of JavaScript helps Internet-based software keep pace with the growing demand.

In addition, web applications such as calendars, task reminders, and even budget planning software are becoming popular with the public at large because they are easy to use, mostly free or very inexpensive, and users can access their data from any device with an Internet connection. They are not tied to the computer that physically stores the data. The V8 JavaScript engine provides developers the power to give users the speed they demand from these types of web applications.

Yellow Box If you're interested in testing V8's speed against other JavaScript engines, either alone, or as part of a web browser, you can do that by following the instructions in the Benchmark section of the Google Code website, http://code.google.com/apis/v8/benchmarks.html.

Like WebKit, Chromium, and Chrome, V8 is also released under the open source license. And what's more, the V8 developers intentionally designed it to be portable. You can take V8 and embed it in any application that requires a JavaScript engine.

V8 gives you the fastest, most stable JavaScript engine available today, and since it's open source, it will remain on the cutting edge of technology and give developers and users the flexibility and speed they need to run the most advanced web applications both today and tomorrow.

MANIPULATING V8 IN THE OPEN SOURCE

If you want to play around with V8's source code, you can find complete instructions on Google Code's page entitled, How to Download and Build V8 at http://code.google.com/apis/v8/build.html.

You can talk to other developers in the V8 forum http://groups.google.com/group/v8-users, or, contribute to the V8 Wiki at **http://code.google.com/p/v8/w/list**.

Shifting Gears: How Gears Works with Chrome

Gears adds several important features that give Chrome added built-in functionality that allows web applications to look and act like local desktop applications. Like all the other components of Chrome, Gears is open source and available to developers. Originally created by Google as Google Gears, this *API* adds a unique flexibility to web applications.

Gears enables standard web apps to

- Create database and web page storage on the user's computer
- Allow the user to create a shortcut to the application directly on her desktop
- Handle batch uploads
- Provide information specific to your location
- Increase web application performance speed

geek speak   *API* stands for *Application Programming Interface*. This is a set of commands that allow a developer to access functions in one program from within another program. Think of it as a set of hooks that allow the programmer to join the functions of two programs.

Let's look at what each of these functions does for both the user and the developer.

Gears Database API and LocalServer API allow applications to create and store database and web pages on the user's computer. These functions are probably the two most important and versatile functions for Gears because they allow programmers to develop web applications that the user can use both online and offline. For example, if you use Gears with Google Docs or *Remember The Milk*, you have the ability to create, access, and edit your documents or to-do list when you're offline. When you go back online, these applications both update the online versions to match the offline versions so they are kept in sync, and no matter where you are, you have the most up-to-date version.

When you want to access a program quickly, desktop shortcuts are the way to go. With a double- or single-click, depending on your settings, the program you want to use opens. Local desktop applications automatically give you the option of adding a desktop shortcut when you install the program. Now, with Gears you can have that same option for your web apps.

 geek speak   *Remember The Milk* is a web application that allows you to create and store your to-do lists online. You'll find it at www.rememberthemilk.com.

Most of the time, when you need to upload several files to the same website you have to upload each file individually. This is time consuming and repetitive. Gears allows the user to select several files, or a batch of files, and upload them all at once.

The user can turn on geolocation capabilities within Chrome. This API allows websites such as search engines and online maps to access information about the user's location so the user gets back more relevant information from his search. For example, if a user is traveling and she searches for Thai restaurants within an online mapping application using geolocation, the results highlight those restaurants closest to her location. It is possible for the user to choose to have the API monitor location continuously, or only once. Furthermore, this feature is turned off by default to prevent security problems. It must be activated by the user.

The WorkerPool API ensures updates and data synchronization between the web application and user computer is handled behind the scenes, when the computer is not actively doing something else. This ensures these features don't slow down the user computer.

For users, these features mean greater flexibility to access the applications they want when and where they need them. Users no longer have a reason to shy away from regular web application use because of concerns about not being able to find an Internet connection. In addition, Gears gives users continuity of use. They can use the same application whether they are online or offline, using their desktop computer at home, using a laptop on a Wi-Fi network, or even using a web-enabled mobile device.

Developers gain the ability to easily create faster, more powerful, and completely portable web applications.

There's been a lot of talk about Google's malware and phishing lists, and how these lists affect web development. Some developers are concerned Google will blacklist websites based on random criteria and ultimately hurt legitimate websites. This fear is really unfounded. The Safe Browsing API included with Google Chrome downloads two published lists to define malware and phishing sites. These lists, goog-black-hash and goog-malware-hash, are consulted by the Safe Browsing API every time the user enters a URL into the Omnibox.

Many wonder where these lists come from. Google works in conjunction with StopBadware.org and antiphishing.org to define the guidelines for being included in these lists. Some things that get you on the malware lists include having a large number of pop-ups, failing to ask permission before downloading or installing software, transferring user data to unidentified locations, being deceptive as to the information or applications your website contains, or purposely taking advantage of known security problems with specific operating systems that may be running user computers. In addition, any software your site offers must be clearly identified, easily and completely removed, and must not link to any other website or application that purposely or accidentally breaks these rules.

Yellow Box

The best course of action for any developer is to stay off these lists; however, if your website has been blacklisted, there are two ways to request a review.

Log in to your Google Webmaster Tools and navigate to the Overview page; then select Request a Review.

Go to the Badware Website Clearinghouse and do a search for your site. Click Request Review, fill in the requested information, and submit the form.

8

Closing the Door

Chrome developers have done everything possible to make Chrome easy for users as well as for developers. Their ideal browser is one that is secure, fast, and able to handle multiple JavaScript chunks efficiently without bogging down. In addition, it was important to Google that Chrome embark upon creating a universal platform on which developers can streamline website, web application, and gadget development. WebKit and V8 have given us such a browser.

In Chapter 9, we look at some of the bookmarklets and add-ons currently available for Chrome. We talk about how to find and install add-ons, and you learn the basics of creating your own.

Spit-Shining Chrome

You have a firm understanding of what Chrome is and how it works, so now you're looking for ways to maximize your productivity, drive users to your website, and, ultimately, increase your bottom line. Add-ons and the tools used to create them can help you do just that. And if you play your cards right, you'll look smarter, faster, and stronger than your competition, too.

Chrome. Better. Faster. Stronger

Google Chrome is a great web browser. It's fast, secure, and easy to use, but for many something is missing: the ability to pick and choose small add-on programs that extend the browser's functionality. Yes, I'm talking about browser extensions. Google began supporting extensions in May 2009.

It took a long time to get here, but you can bet it was worth the wait. Chrome extensions let you do more with your browser. Activities such as blocking ads, parental control of children's Internet usage, monitoring current weather and storm watches or warnings, and many other things can now be done right from your Chrome browser.

One of the reasons it took so long to get extensions was that Google wanted to make sure they got it right. Google had a long list of goals that had to be met by the extension system.

For starters Google wanted the Chrome extension system to support many different API styles so programmers didn't have to worry about programming extensions specifically for Chrome. They wanted the system to be something the Chrome team could create once, without having to spend a lot of time updating it. And, they didn't want the user to have to worry about updates either. Chrome's extension system updates itself quietly in the background just like Chrome does. There's no need to disable and reenable extensions when Chrome updates.

In addition, the Chrome extension system is secure. One of the concerns of the Chrome team was that hackers or malware not be able to gain access through the API port. Extensions aren't given blanket security approval. They only get the permissions they need to run, ensuring the security of your system. Also, in the interest of security, extensions are executed in their own sandboxes, just like tabs and dangerous extensions can be blacklisted for all Chrome and Chromium browsers, just like malicious websites.

Chrome extensions also support content scripts. These are small JavaScript files, similar to those that Greasemonkey uses. However, unlike Greasemonkey, content scripts run in the Google Chrome extension system give the user the ability to:

- **Include Cascading Style Sheets**—CSS support gives you the power to completely change the appearance of a website using a uniform style sheet for the entire site.

- **Include multiple files**—This lets you run more than one script for every web page the browser loads. For example, you can change the font size and replace all images on a page with an image of your own choosing.

■ **Run scripts at the beginning or the end of page load**—By default, scripts run after the web page is loaded into Chrome. You do, however, have the ability to run your scripts at the beginning, instead. Simply add "run_at": "document_start" to your content script.

> **geek speak**
>
> *Greasemonkey* is an extension originally developed for Mozilla Firefox that lets the user run small lines of JavaScript to add features to, or change the appearance of, a website. Greasemonkey is explained in greater depth in the next section of this chapter.

Along with the extension system comes the ability to support NPAPI plug-ins. Developed by Netscape, NPAPI (Netscape Plugin Application Programming Interface) is the most common plug-in architecture used today. NPAPI plug-ins are used widely in Firefox, Safari, Opera, Konqueror, and some versions of Internet Explorer. It's also, of course, used in Google Chrome. NPAPI plug-ins are compatible with Microsoft Windows, Mac, and Linux operating systems.

Plug-ins are small programs designed to handle specific types of files encountered on the Internet. Real Player, Adobe Flash Player, and Adobe Acrobat are popular plug-ins that handle video files, web animation, and PDF files, respectively.

You can find more information on the extensions currently available by checking out the official Google Blog at http://googleblog.blogspot.com or the Chromium Development Documentation at http://dev.chromium.org/Home.

...Extended Chrome's Functionality

Even though Google Chrome is fairly new, the open source community has jumped at Google's challenge to help build a better mousetrap. Within weeks of release, programmers all over the world developed pieces of code intended to improve the look and add to the functionality of Google Chrome. One reason for this is the popularity of the well-known web browser Firefox by Mozilla. Firefox is a good core browser that is greatly enhanced by the hundreds of open source add-ons and themes available. These add-ons enable Firefox to do just about anything, which is great, but at the same time it's just not as fast as Chrome. However, to the hundreds of thousands of Firefox users worldwide, a few seconds of extra speed may not be worth giving up functionality they've come to depend on.

The way to solve this, of course, is to develop add-ons and themes for Google Chrome to combine lightning fast speed with unmatched versatility.

Gears

One of the most powerful add-ons associated with Chrome is Gears.

But wait, you say? Gears isn't an add-on; it's part of Chrome.

Well yes, it is, but it's also an add-on. When you're using Chrome, Gears is an included component. There's no need for you to install anything. But Gears is an added component for other browsers. If you use any other browser and want to use Gears, you have to download and install the correct version of Gears for your browser and platform. That makes Gears an add-on for those browsers. Since Gears was developed by Google, they saw fit to include it in Chrome.

Once you begin using Google Gears, you may well come to rely on the added functionality it provides. Features like offline access to your Gmail and Google Docs accounts are handy and give you the ability to continue working on important projects in the event your Internet service is interrupted. You can even install Google Gears on your laptop, netbook, or mobile phone device for those times you are away from an Internet connection.

Gears is available regardless of which operating system you use. Windows XP and Vista users can install Gears in either Firefox or Internet Explorer. Mac users have their choice of Firefox or Safari versions, and Linux users can install Gears in Firefox. You can also put Gears on your *Windows Mobile* or *Android* powered mobile device.

Windows Mobile is the operating system for mobile devices put out by Microsoft.

Android is a mobile device operating system by Google.

Gears is fast and easy to install. You can find it here: http://gears.google.com. When you land on the Gears page, it should automatically read your operating system and browser. Click the blue **Install Gears** button, read the Terms of Service, and decide whether you want Gears to send reports to Google in case of a crash. When you click **Agree and Download**, the Gears installer asks whether you want to Run or Save. Select **Run**. When the installer is finished, just restart your browser.

The power of Gears shines through if you're a web application user or developer. Gears is truly unmatched for providing users with excellent flexibility whether working online or offline. Gears API allows users to use specific web applications when working offline. By saving a copy of the application and archiving copies of your documents, you have access to files and documents you created on the Internet using web applications. Also, Gears give your web apps the capability to integrate with the user's operating system. Web apps look and act more like a natively installed program. As if that wasn't enough, Gears also lets websites store important information directly on your hard drive, in a fully searchable database, so you can access your information quickly and easily. And, finally, the capability to run JavaScript in the background provides an easy way for developers to safely add experimental functions to the web browser without having to completely revamp the browser.

The benefits of these features can be best illustrated by example.

Google Docs is a web application that allows users to create written documents using a fully featured online word processor. Google Docs is compatible with most locally based word processing document formats, including .doc, .odt, and .pdf. It's a great tool that allows you to work on projects anywhere you have an Internet connection.

But what happens if you lose your Internet connection, or you need to access an important document from a meeting where you don't have Internet access? That's where Gears comes in. As long as you have offline syncing turned on, you're covered. Gears automatically saves the most current copy of your online documents locally. Just click the Google Docs icon on your desktop or Quick Start bar, and Docs opens and gives you access to all your documents. You can create new documents, edit old ones, save, and print. The only functions you won't have access to are things such as online collaboration, which requires an Internet connection.

Here are some web applications that use Gears to give you offline access:

- **Remember The Milk**—An online task manager that lets you organize tasks with lists and tags, set due dates and reminders, and even schedule repeated tasks (www.rememberthemilk.com).

- **Google Reader**—An RSS reader you can use to manage and read your favorite blogs and news subscriptions. When used with Gears, you can read the last 2,000 posts while you're offline. You can also tag or star posts for later reference (www.reader.google.com).

- **Zoho**—An online office productivity suite developed by AdventNet, Inc. Gears lets you view and edit your Zoho documents when you're not connected to the Internet (www.zoho.com).

■ **MindMeister**—An online mind mapping application. When used with Gears, you have the full ability to view, edit, and create mind maps. Your data is stored locally and automatically updated to your online account the next time you log in (www.mindmeister.com/).

■ **PassPack**—A password manager that gives you the ability to download your passwords and change them from your local computer. You can easily sync your local and online PassPack account by using the program's backup and restore capabilities (www.passpack.com).

■ **Buxfer**—An online personal money manager that gives you access to your financial information whether you're online or offline (www.buxfer.com).

■ **Autodesk Labs Project Draw**—A drawing program that uses Google Gears to give you complete offline ability to create and edit your diagrams (www.draw.labs.autodesk.com).

■ **Picasa**—An online photo storage and editing application. When used with Gears, you can view your online stored photos while offline (www.picasa.google.com).

■ **Paymo**—An online time tracker that lets you easily track your time so you can bill clients, or just be aware of the time you spend on specific projects (www.paymo.biz).

■ **MySpace**—Search and sort your MySpace messages offline (www.myspace.com).

■ **WordPress**—A blogging client which uses Gears to add speed to your blogging (www.wordpress.com).

Bookmarklets

Developed by the open source community, bookmarklets are tools to give you additional functions. These unofficial add-ons work differently than what you may be used to with other browsers. Bookmarklets are just that—little chunks of JavaScript code saved in your Chrome bookmarks. If you install them in the Bookmarks bar as opposed to in the Other Bookmarks folder, you'll have your bookmarklets at your fingertips.

These bookmarklets provide the added features many users have come to rely on from their web browsers. If you use social website sharing services such as Digg or StumbleUpon, you may miss the lack of one-click sharing you've grown accustomed to in other browsers. With bookmarklets, you simply plunk the code into your bookmarks and immediately have access to your Digg, StumbleUpon, or Delicious features. Same for Twitter addicts. You don't have to give up your favorite sites.

Here's where you'll find some of the most popular bookmarklets. Note that these bookmarklets are constantly being upgraded. Since installation instructions sometimes change, be sure to follow the instructions given by the developer.

- **Google Toolbar for Chrome**—One of the best and most comprehensive bookmarklet sets, this is targeted to web developers and webmasters and gives you specific functions. You can validate HTML and CSS with the W3C, get the date a page was last modified, highlight all links on a page, auto lookup all mentions of your page on Technorati or Digg, perform a domain lookup, count the number of links on a page, automatically make all URLs clickable, open all links on the page in new tabs, and even remove all background music, Flash, or Java, from a given page (http://www.chromeplugins.org/google/chrome-tips-tricks/google-toolbar-chrome-50.html).

- **Digg**—Add websites to Digg with the click of a link (http://skattertech.com/2006/06/digg-this-bookmarklet/). Drag the Digg logo onto your Chrome Bookmark bar.

- **ChromeStumble**—Gives you basic access to your StumbleUpon account. For this one to work, you have to have StumbleUpon installed and set to log in automatically on Firefox (http://code.google.com/p/chromestumble/).

- **Twitlet**—Lets you update your Twitter tweets without logging in to Twitter (http://www.twitlet.com/).

- **TwitThis**—Lets you send a message through Twitter about the web page you're currently viewing. This site contains several versions of TwitThis, so be sure to look for the Bookmarklet link and instructions (http://twitthis.com/).

- **Dual Pane View**—Allows you to view websites split screen in Chrome. This one is great if you need to compare documents (http://www.chromeplugins.org/plugins/google-chrome-dual-view/).

- **Gmail This**—Lets you email anyone using your Gmail account without leaving the page you're on. The easiest way to get this one is from an About.com page. Follow the simple install instructions (http://email.about.com/library/misc/blgmail_this_bookmarklet.htm).

- **Search Selected Text**—A batch of bookmarklets that let you perform a search for specific text using a variety of search engines without changing web pages. There are several of these on the Chrome Plugins website (http://www.chromeplugins.org/chrome/search-selected-text-with-google-chrome/).

- **ChromeMailer**—Gives you the ability to use the mailto link on a website without logging in to your Gmail account. This is useful if you are replying to a classified ad or otherwise want to send an email directly from a website (http://skaelede.hu/?e=chromemailer&lg=en/).

.exe Tools

Unlike bookmarklets, an .exe tool is a small, standalone executable program that performs a limited function. These programs work with Google Chrome to give you features not normally found in a web browser. Here are a few must-have .exe tools developed to extend the functionality of Google Chrome and simplify daily tasks.

- **TabsLock**—Open Google Chrome with the Caps Lock key on your keyboard (http://tabslock.com).

- **ChromePass**—View vital saved password information. If you've ever forgotten a password, you know just how frustrating it can be, not to mention the potential work time lost while you wait for the website to reset your password. This .exe tool solves this problem by giving you access to view origin URL, action URL, username, password, and time created for each password stored by Google Chrome (http://www.nirsoft.net/utils/chromepass.html).

- **Google Chrome Backup**—Create, manage, and store profiles for your Google Chrome browser. Each person who uses your computer can have his own Google Chrome Profile so that history and bookmarks are separate (http://www.parhelia-tools.com/products/gcb/googlechrome.aspx).

- **Chrome Privacy Guard (CPG)**— Anonymize Chrome's RLZ reporting. If you're bothered by the RLZ reporting that Chrome insists on, you can install this tool, which deletes the unique ID each time you start Chrome, so you can keep your privacy. This tool was originally created in German. You can download the English version from http://blog.gjl-network.net/blog/index.php?archives/166-English.html.

- **Chrome Automatic Theme Switcher**—Themes let you change the color, icons, or fonts displayed on your screen. There are quite a few themes for Google Chrome, and often they're difficult to manage and change. This tool makes it easier to manage your Chrome themes. This one's a little rough around the edges, so be sure to read the forum notes (http://chromespot.com/showthread.php?t=266).

- **AutoHotKey**—If you miss the simplicity of keyboard shortcuts that you get with other browsers, try this tool to set your own keyboard shortcuts. You can specify shortcuts for common tasks, such as changing tabs, closing tabs, undoing the last closed tab, and going forward and backward through your browsing history (http://www.autohotkey.com/).

- **Google Chrome Bookmark Exporter**—Use this add-on to export your Chrome bookmarks into an HTML file that you can then import into any other browser (http://www.googlechromeboard.com/export-google-chrome-bookmarks-t78.html).

Themes and Theme Editors

Themes give you the ability to change the look and feel of your computer. The most common type of theme consists of several image and DLL files that specify how Chrome should display the background, font, and icons. More complicated themes also let you change your computer's wallpaper, screensaver, icons, and system sounds.

Browser themes do the same thing, but for your web browser. One popular browser has hundreds of themes created by the open source community. You can even decorate your browser for Christmas, Hanukkah, Eid-al-Fitr, or any other holiday you fancy.

Currently, the themes available for Chrome are a bit sparse. A few holiday and cartoon character-based themes are available, and you'll find a respectable number of themes to let you change Chrome's color. I'm sure as Chrome develops and matures, the number and quality of themes will increase dramatically. In Chapter 10, "Making It Yours," we show you two ways to make your own simple theme for Chrome.

For now, here's where you can find themes you can download and install. Like any program you download from the Internet, read any accompanying documentation or install instructions, and if available, any comments about the theme. Some of these themes have been created by programmers well known in the open source community, while others are offered by comparative strangers.

- **ChromeSpot**—Offers a good number of themes for your use (http://chromespot.com/forumdisplay.php?f=19).

- **Chrome Plugins**—We saw this site in the previous section. This is also a great site if you're looking for themes. Be sure to explore the site to see what else it offers (http://www.chromeplugins.org/category/themes/).

- **Themes for Chrome**—This one only offers themes, although there are a decent number of them (http://www.themesforchrome.com).

- **Chromium Themes**—We saved the best for last (http://sites.google.com/site/chromiumthemes/).

With all these themes, you need a way to manage them. Theme managers give you an easy way to store, sort through, delete, and apply downloaded themes to your browser. There are several theme managers available for Chrome, one of the most comprehensive is available at http://sites.google.com/site/chromiumthemes/beta/tutorials/chromium-theme-manager.

Now that you've seen what other people are doing, and you've downloaded, installed, and played with a few themes, you might want to edit a current theme or even create your own. There are several ways to edit a theme. One way is to open the source code and change the color, or the *PNG file* associated with the theme.

geek speak   *PNG files* refer to a format of graphics. Portable Network Graphics are commonly used in artwork for the Web.

For now, here are two theme builders for you to play with:

- A far easier way is to use a theme editor like the one on psyToy.net (http://psytoy.net/everything-else/google-chrome-theme-editor/.

- Or this one: http://chromespot.com/showthread.php?t=851.

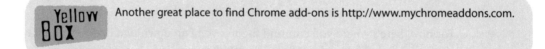

Yellow Box   Another great place to find Chrome add-ons is http://www.mychromeaddons.com.

Greasemonkey

Chrome users familiar with Firefox probably know about Greasemonkey, which gives the browser the ability to run small bits of JavaScript to change the way HTML is rendered on-the-fly. When you have Greasemonkey installed, it loads in your browser first, before any HTML is loaded, and runs any scripts you may have installed for the page you are loading. These scripts let you rearrange your favorite (or not so favorite) websites. Use it to remove sidebars, customize buttons, or even remove banner ads. Like all the other applications and programs we've talked about, Greasemonkey is open source.

Support for Greasemonkey is built into Chrome, so you don't have to install it. However, you do have to enable it. To enable Greasemonkey, right-click on the **Chrome shortcut** on your desktop and select **Properties**. As shown in Figure 9.1, make sure the Shortcut tab is selected and change the target line to look like this:

```
C:\Users\Aaron's\AppData\Local\Google\Chrome\Application\chrome.exe
➥-enable-greasemonkey
```

Some computers may require you to put the line in quotation marks.

Click **Apply**, then close the window and restart Chrome.

FIGURE 9.1
Here's how the Properties window should look when you're done.

Now that Greasemonkey is enabled, just save your scripts in the C:\Scripts folder. Unless you've used Greasmonkey before, you'll probably have to create this folder. To do this, Open **My Computer** (**Computer** on Windows Vista or 7), select the drive letter that corresponds to your hard drive—usually C:. Now, right-click anywhere in the window and select **New**, **Folder**. Name the new folder, **Scripts**, and press **Enter** on your keyboard.

When you write a new script, save it in this folder, and Greasemonkey finds and runs the script each time you run Chrome.

Always write your Greasemonkey scripts in a text editor such as Notepad. To save JavaScript files in Notepad simply click the arrow at the end of the **Save as type** menu, and select **All Files** from the drop-down menu as illustrated in Figure 9.2.

FIGURE 9.2

Configure Notepad to save JavaScript, or any other file extension with just one click.

Next, name your file and include the file extension .js to designate it as a JavaScript file. Figure 9.3 shows the file named Script01.js, but you should use names that describe the function of the script. For example, if your JavaScript file removes all the images on a page and replaces them with your favorite quotation, you could consider naming the file imagetoquote.js.

When you're finished, click **Save**.

It's that simple. Greasemonkey scripts for Chrome are easy to write. And in Chapter 10, you learn how to write a basic script. It's easier if you have an understanding of JavaScript, but even if you've never touched the language, you can easily learn enough to start writing scripts for Greasemonkey.

If you're not inclined to write your own, that's okay, too. You can find a large number of scripts written by others at userscripts.org. The great thing about this repository is most scripts are tagged for the browser for which they're designed. Not every script in the repository works with Chrome. You want to look for those scripts that are tagged for either Chrome or Safari. Scripts developed for other browsers may work with Google Chrome, but they may do things you don't expect. Like all open source software, be sure to read all accompanying comments and documentation.

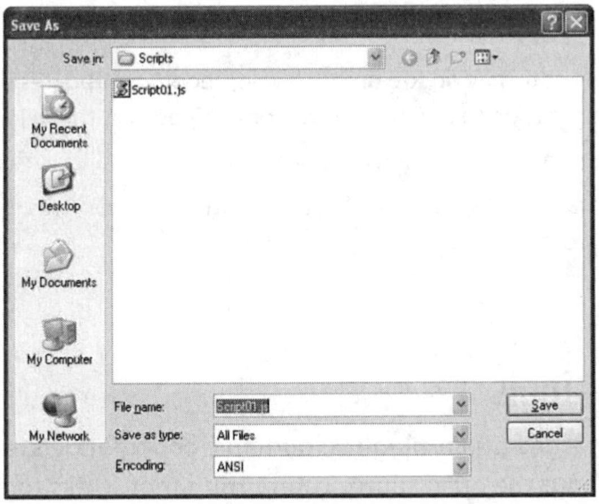

FIGURE 9.3
Always remember to use the file extension .js when saving JavaScript files.

Greasemetal

When Chrome was first released Greasemonkey wasn't yet supported. Greasemetal was created by a Japanese developer while researching for a Japanese public software company. Like its better known predecessor, this standalone program runs user scripts developed in the JavaScript language.

While it's not as widely known, Greasemetal recognizes and executes the same scripts as Greasemonkey. You can use the website in the section discussing Greasemonkey to find and download scripts for Greasemetal. So, unlike users of other browsers, Chrome users have a choice in script execution.

To install Greasemetal, first download the program from http://greasemetal.31tools.com/.

After the program installs, close Google Chrome, and start Greasemetal. It opens Chrome and executes the setup. Now you can start adding user scripts. Download scripts from userscripts.org, or write your own. Save scripts to C:\Documents and Settings\<*username*>\My Documents\userjs in Windows

XP. If you're using Windows Vista or 7, save in C:\Users\<*username*>\ Documents\userjs.

Remember that while you have a choice between Greasemetal and Greasemonkey, you do need to use either one or the other. You can't run both at the same time. Take some time to try out each one separately and decide which you like better.

Yellow Box   If you want to stay on top of the development and updates of Greasemonkey or Greasemetal, you'll find their development pages at the following websites.
Greasemonkey: http://www.greasespot.net/
Greasemetal: http://greasemetal.31tools.com/ and http://labs.cybozu.co.jp/blog/ kazuhoatwork/

We Have the Tools

You've learned about plug-ins, add-ons, bookmarklets, and .exe tools. We've talked about the open source community that works together to create all these great programs. In Chapter 10 we show you how to create your own bookmarklets, add-ons, and even your own theme for Chrome, so you can begin to join the open source community that will help define this great browser. But, first we need to talk about the programming tools and languages used to create Chrome add-ons. Teaching these languages in depth is beyond the scope of this book, but this section gives you a basic understanding of the programming languages you need.

Libraries

Libraries are repositories of open source code that programmers can examine, change, and insert into their own projects. Google Chrome is, of course, built from open source libraries. These libraries are included in the source code for anyone who wants to tear it apart and look for them. The advantage of having access to the libraries is that you can change the code in the library to change the way Google Chrome works and functions. For example, one gentleman used the code in the zlib to change the way data is compressed. Taking advantage of these libraries can reduce your coding time and give you solid working code to use and tweak as needed. Plus, if you're new to programming, you can use these libraries as a good starting point to see how code is put together to form a program.

More than 25 different libraries are included in the Google Chrome web browser. We walk you through the navigation of one library. All these libraries are hosted on chromium.org pages and have the same format and site functions. You find a full list of the libraries, their function, and their URL in Table 9.1 at the end of this section.

Libjpg is the programming library that tells your computer how to handle items in the jpeg and jfif formats. Remember from Chapter 8, "Developing Sites for Chrome," that jpeg is a format type used for graphics, such as photos or drawings. You find the repository libjpg for Google Chrome at http://src.chromium.org/viewvc/chrome/trunk/src/third_party/libjpeg/?dir_pagestart=0.

As you can see in Figure 9.4, this page is like a table of contents for the library. The first column is the File column. Here, each filename is listed. Files are listed first by type of file and then by age of the file. For example, you can see that the third and fourth entries are both README files. If you look at the third column, you can see that the first README is older than the second.

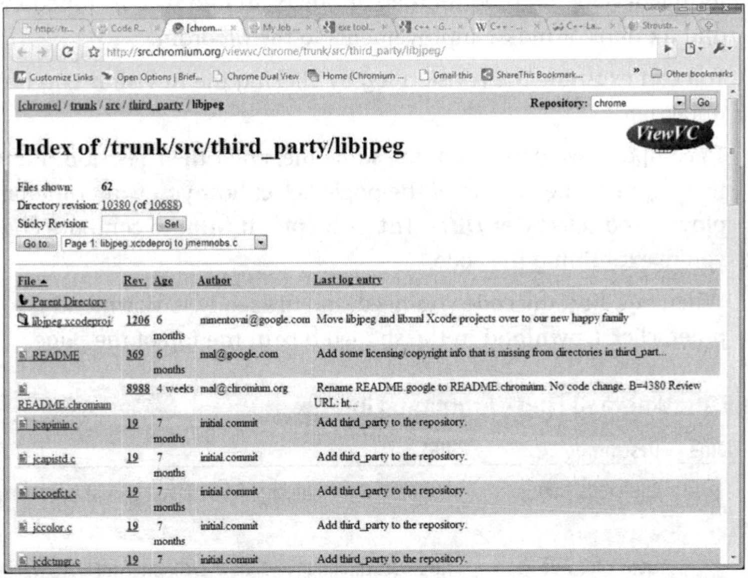

FIGURE 9.4

It is easy to navigate the jpeg library.

If you want to reverse this listing and list the newer files on top of the older files, click the column header, **Age**. All columns can be modified in this manner.

The second column is the revision number. For most files, you only see the most recent revision.

The third column tells you the age of the file, or how long that particular revision has been in use.

The Author column tells you who uploaded the file and who gets credit for creating that revision. Sometimes the author is listed as an email address, and other times as a nickname.

Last Log Entry gives you an idea of what function the code performs.

If you scroll to the bottom of the page, you see a link on the right side of your screen. ViewVC Help takes you to a help page.

To view code for a specific file, click the link in the **Rev** column. You can view but not edit the code. This allows you to read over and make sure this is the chunk of code you need before you download. Most developers use programming notes to explain what each section of code is supposed to do. In many languages, these developers notes, or dev notes, are placed in between the symbols /* Your note or explanation goes here*/. These notes make it easier for the developing programmer, or others, to find specific functions to locate and fix bugs or make improvements to the program.

You can examine the revision log by clicking the **Revision Log** link in the upper-left.

To compare two versions of the same file, enter their revision numbers in the text boxes at the bottom of the page. Select how you want differences displayed and select **Get Diffs**. This is helpful if want to compare changes as you're examining the code.

When you find the code you need and are ready to download it to your computer, click **Download** in the shaded box at the top of the page.

Table 9.1   Where to Find Chromium Libraries

Library Name	Description	URL
Google Breakpad	Crash reporting	http://src.chromium.org/viewvc/chrome/trunk/src/breakpad/
WebKit	Library for WebKit	http://src.chromium.org/viewvc/chrome/trunk/src/webkit/
Google v8	Library for the V8 JavaScript Engine	http://code.google.com/p/v8/source/browse
Network Security Systems or NSS	Support for security applications across different operating systems	http://src.chromium.org/viewvc/chrome/trunk/src/third_party/npapi/

Library Name	Description	URL
TLS Lite	Python library for testing	http://src.chromium.org/viewvc/chrome/trunk/src/third_party/tlslite/
Sqlite	Self contained, serverless database	http://src.chromium.org/viewvc/chrome/trunk/src/third_party/sqlite/
Zlib	Data compression	http://src.chromium.org/viewvc/chrome/trunk/src/third_party/zlib/
LZMA	Default compression method for 7z format	http://src.chromium.org/viewvc/chrome/trunk/src/third_party/lzma_sdk/
Libpng	Support for PNG files	http://src.chromium.org/viewvc/chrome/trunk/src/third_party/libpng/
Libjpg	Support for JPEG and JFIF files	http://src.chromium.org/viewvc/chrome/trunk/src/third_party/libjpeg/
Bsdiff	Libraries for applying patches to binary files	http://src.chromium.org/viewvc/chrome/trunk/src/third_party/bsdiff/
Bspatch	More libraries for binary file patches	http://src.chromium.org/viewvc/chrome/trunk/src/third_party/bspatch/
Skia	Renders vector graphics	http://src.chromium.org/viewvc/chrome/trunk/src/skia/
NSPR	Non-operating system- specific API	http://src.chromium.org/viewvc/chrome/trunk/src/base/third_party/nspr/
Hunspell	Spell checker library	http://src.chromium.org/viewvc/chrome/trunk/src/chrome/third_party/hunspell/
Google C++ Testing Framework	Writing applications in C++ for Linux, Windows, and Mac	http://code.google.com/p/googletest/downloads/list
Pthreads-w32	API for multithreaded application	http://src.chromium.org/viewvc/chrome/trunk/src/third_party/pthread/
Scons	Open Source application building tool	http://src.chromium.org/viewvc/chrome/trunk/src/third_party/scons/
stringencoders	Tool for encoding and decoding data sent or received over the Internet	http://src.chromium.org/viewvc/chrome/trunk/src/third_party/modp_b64/
Windows template library	C++ specific to Microsoft Windows applications	http://src.chromium.org/viewvc/chrome/trunk/src/chrome/third_party/wtl/

Continues

Table 9.1 Continued

Library Name	Description	URL
Bzip2	File compression	http://src.chromium.org/viewvc/chrome/trunk/src/third_party/bzip2/
Libxml	Understanding and translating XML	http://src.chromium.org/viewvc/chrome/trunk/src/third_party/libxml/
libxslt	Support for XLS transforms	http://src.chromium.org/viewvc/chrome/trunk/src/third_party/libxslt/
Netscape Plugin Application Programming Interface or NPAPI	Multi-operating plugin system	http://src.chromium.org/viewvc/chrome/trunk/src/third_party/npapi/

C++

If you want to tweak the source code for Google Chrome, you need a thorough understanding of the language in which it's written. First developed in 1979 by Bjarne Stroustrup, C++ was designed to be a statically typed, free-form, midlevel programming language versatile enough to handle object-oriented, procedural, data abstraction, and generic programming styles. This level of flexibility allows the developer to choose the best programming style for the job.

C++ is compiled into machine language. Different types of compilers are needed for the various computer chipsets.

Many great books have been written on programming with C++, including by its creator, Mr. Bjarne Strousttrup. If you want to gain a complete understanding of C++, we suggest you start with those.

One of the best ways to learn how a programming language works is to tear apart some code and examine it. And that's exactly what we're going to do—examine a chunk of code that makes up Chromium. We go through the code line-by-line and talk about what it does. Once you get comfortable with C++ you'll be able to make changes in the way Chrome operates.

The following code listings come from the base library. This particular chunk identifies the computer CPU so the compiler knows to which version of machine language it should compile. The CPU information is stored in a piece of memory called "string."

```
// Copyright (c) 2006-2008 The Chromium Authors. All rights reserved.
// Use of this source code is governed by a BSD-style license that can
// be found in the LICENSE file.
```

This section identifies the owner/developer of the code and specifies the type of license the code is released under. It also tells you where to find the full license.

```
#ifndef BASE_CPU_H_
```

This line translates into English as, "If item called Base_CPU_H is not defined." `if` is the beginning of an `if` statement. `n`, stands for not/negative—in computer speak, null—and `def` means defined. The rest of the code tells the computer what to do if BASE_CPU_H is not defined. In C++ programming, every `if` statement must end with an `endif`.

```
#define BASE_CPU_H_
```

Define BASE_CPU_H. When you put these two lines together, you get "if BASE_CPU_H is not defined, then define it."

```
#include <string>
```

Include the library called "string" and insert it here. The string library is defined elsewhere in the program; this code chunk calls that library into use here. The string library is a separate chunk of code that tells the computer how to handle text forms.

```
namespace base {
```

Namespace is where all the standard elements of C++ are defined. So, this line says go to `namespace` and define `base`. Base is what the program will call this instance of namespace.

```
// Query information about the processor.
class CPU {
```

This is a note so the developer knows what the following code does. Programmers use notes frequently to make it easier to track down and fix bugs in the code. In C++ all notes are preceded by the symbols //.

`Class CPU {` creates a type of C++ object, called a class. The name of this particular class is CPU.2 The code between the brackets defines this new class.

```
 public:
```

This simply means I'm going to tell you to create something, and when you do, allow all parts of the whole program to access and use it.

```
 // Constructor
 CPU();
```

Constructor is the programmer's note. In this case, a constructor named CPU is created. A constructor creates the item that we just defined and () tells C++ this is a function.

```
// Accessors for CPU information.
```

This is a developer's note stating that the following code defines the accessors for the CPU information. An accessor is a way to access data without changing it. Accessors look at and work with data, but don't make any changes to the data.

```
const std::string& vendor_name() const { return cpu_vendor_; }
int stepping() const { return stepping_; }
int model() const { return model_; }
int family() const { return family_; }
int type() const { return type_; }
int extended_model() const { return ext_model_; }
int extended_family() const { return ext_family_; }
```

This chunk talks to the CPU and gathers the data needed to identify the type of computer chip. Each piece of data is defined as part of the following code. int is shorthand for integer, and tells the computer that the data between the parentheses is an integer, and const, is shorthand for constant. This defines the data between the brackets as something that cannot be changed.

```
private:// Query the processor for CPUID information.
void Initialize();int type_;   // process type
int family_;   // family of the processor
int model_;   // model of processor
int stepping_;   // processor revision number
int ext_model_;
int ext_family_;
std::string cpu_vendor_;
```

This section defines each piece of data for the programmer. Remember, the symbols // indicate programming notes.

```
};
}   // namespace base
#endif   // BASE_CPU_H_
```

This chunk ends the program. In programming, each bracketed function must have an end bracket, and each if statement must have an endif. This concludes the routine called BASE_CPU_H.

This program is just one small piece of the code that makes up Google Chrome. There are hundreds of these short, direct programs, called routines, that work together to create many of the applications you use every day.

There's not enough code here for you to learn C++ from, however this small program should give you an idea of what C++ looks like, and how it works.

JavaScript

JavaScript is an ideal scripting language for building browser applications. It's normally used on server machines to tell the client computer or Internet user machine to perform a specific task. Every web browser understands JavaScript, and the absolute speed of V8 eliminates the frustrating runtime delays. Speed of execution at run-time means your web applications won't slow down each time the user executes a command.

JavaScript was developed by Brendan Eich, under the original name of Mocha. At that time, Mr. Eich worked for Netscape, and after several name changes Mocha was released with Netscape Navigator in 1995. Sun Microsystems continues to hold the trademark to the name JavaScript.

Since its release, JavaScript has become one of the most popular scripting languages because it's so flexible and easy to learn. One of the things that makes JavaScript so flexible is that it's executed at runtime. That makes it perfect for things like extending an already compiled program or changing the way web pages are displayed.

JavaScript is used to create scripts for Greasemonkey and Greasemetal, and to develop bookmarklets. Both these scripts are short lines of code. In fact, bookmarklets are less than 2,000 characters.

In Chapter 10, we use JavaScript to build a bookmarklet and a Greasemonkey script.

Closing the Door

Versatility is important in today's Internet. Savvy users expect the ability to completely customize their web browsers. Google Chrome gives you that ability with open source code and the use of add-ons. The open source community as a whole adds to the versatility of Chrome with the development of bookmarklets, .exe tools, and great scripts for Greasemonkey and Greasemetal.

And now, you have the tools to tap into this ever-expanding resource. In Chapter 10, you learn how to create your own theme, build a simple bookmarklet, and build an easy script for Greasemonkey or Greasemetal.

Making It Yours

S o, you installed Greasemonkey or Greasemetal, tried out all the add-ons and bookmarklets, and even played with some themes and color schemes. Do you still need more to make Chrome uniquely yours? Or, maybe you want to stick a timid toe into the open source waters?

Here's how you create your first theme and bring your fledgling bookmarklets or scripts into the world.

You Gotta Have a Theme

Quite a few themes are available for Google Chrome, and more are being uploaded all the time. But if you just can't wait for someone else to make a theme you love, there are several ways to do it yourself.

The most direct, and most difficult, way is to download the Chrome source code and open the image files. Every image you see as part of the Chrome browser is its own image. To create a full theme, you need to edit each and every image. Then you have to compile it all into a .dll file so Chrome can see it. After all that, it's time to load everything into Chrome.

However, that's a lot of work, and if you're not a programmer it can be difficult to locate the files you want and make everything work. The simplest way to create your own Chrome themes is with a little program called Chromium Theme Creator. You find this gem at http://chromespot.com/showthread.php?t=851. The download link is about halfway down the page. Once you've downloaded the installer, click it to run. If you're installing from Chrome, select the arrow in the download bar and choose **Open**. The Setup Wizard looks like the screen in Figure 10.1.

Select **Next** to read through and accept the GNU Free Software license agreement. Follow the prompts to finish program installation.

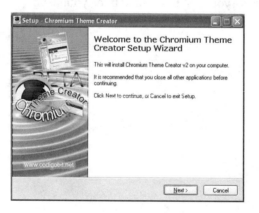

FIGURE 10.1

The Chromium Theme Creator Setup Wizard is easy to use.

If you're using Windows Vista, the first time you start the program, you may get an error message that looks like the one shown in Figure 10.2. Just select **Run as Administrator** to run Chromium Theme Creator.

FIGURE 10.2
Select Run As Administrator if you get this error.

When you open Chromium Theme Creator, you see four tabs: Viewer, Theme Creator, Settings, and About. While the About tab is self-explanatory, we cover each of the other three tabs in the following sections.

Viewer

The Viewer tab lets you preview and apply your themes. By default nine themes are included with the theme creator. On the left, you see a list of theme names along with the Chrome version number for which each theme was developed. Select the theme you want. A preview appears in the window to the right. When you find the theme you want, just select **Apply** (see Figure 10.3).

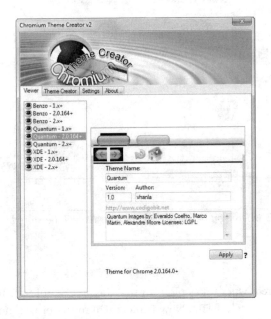

FIGURE 10.3
The Viewer tab lets you preview themes.

Settings

The Settings tab tells the program where to find everything it needs. When you open the Settings tab, you see the paths for Chrome, Theme, and Project have been auto-filled. These are probably correct, and you can leave these setting alone unless you run into problems. However, notice the path for Image Editor is blank. Figure 10.4 shows the Settings tab with default settings.

Before you begin editing images to create your theme, you have to tell Google Theme Creator where to find your image editor. To do this, either type in the path by hand or use the button to the right to browse to your image editor. The image editor you use must support PNG files. Open Office Draw, Photoshop, or Fireworks work fine. After you tell the program where to find your image editor, click **Save Settings**.

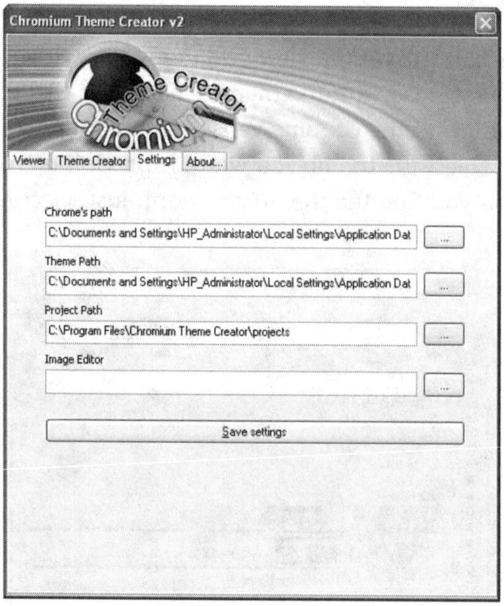

FIGURE 10.4

The Settings tab is where you designate where your file will be stored.

Theme Creator

All the real work takes place in the Theme Creator tab. To start working on a new theme, select **File**, **New Project**. Fill in the project name and other information that helps you identify your project and click **Save**.

The Properties tab simply gives you a place to record version number, author, URL for the theme, and any comments you want users to see. Figure 10.5 shows the Properties tab with some details filled in.

FIGURE 10.5
The Properties tab lets you record author name, version number and any notes for readers.

Under the Viewer tab, you select the part of the browser you want to edit. Just mouse over and click on the section you want to edit. The Explorer tab, as shown in Figure 10.6, opens with your image choices on the left. If you click once on an image, a preview appears in the window to the right. If you double-click on an image, it opens in your image editor. Edit each image you want to include in your theme and save your images as PNG files in the folder indicated by Project Path.

To build your theme, first open your project using Chromium Theme Creator. Now select **File, Build**. Follow the onscreen directions for the version of Chrome you're using and Voilà! Your theme is complete. Figure 10.7 shows a Google page with a theme applied with Chromium Theme Creator. That could not have been easier.

FIGURE 10.6

The Explorer tab lets you choose the image you want to edit.

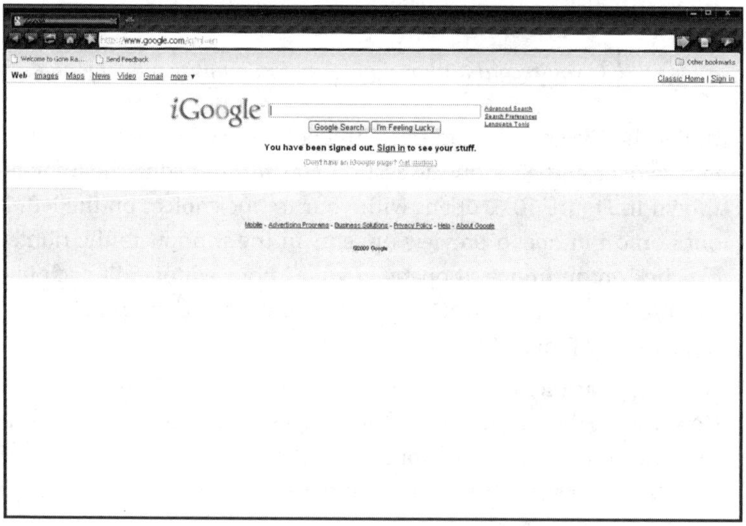

FIGURE 10.7

This is Google with a black theme applied to Chrome.

Just a Little Bookmarklet

As you saw in Chapter 9, "Spit-Shining Chrome," many different book-marklets are available already. We're going to create one that removes banner ads from the web pages you visit. You can use this to customize how all banner ads appear on your computer. You could replace every banner ad with your project list, a photo of your family, or a motivational message or favorite quote. Just remember, whatever you place there can only be seen on your computer when you use Chrome. At the same time, anyone who uses Chrome on your computer will also have banner ads replaced, unless you remove the script.

JavaScript code is written in a text editor, such as Notepad, and must be saved as an HTML file that is, a file with a .html extension that the computer is able to recognize.

Now, take a look at the code:

```
<A HREF='javascript:function%20NoBanner(){
```

This lets the computer know what follows is an HTML link and defines the language as JavaScript. JavaScript code is typically contained within a function. The function is contained within curly braces, so the end of this line is the start of the function. You can't use spaces within bookmarklets, so %20 is used to give separation.

Now, define the variable. For our purposes, the variable "picset" is a collection of all the images displayed on the web page you're viewing. "Document" means the current web page and "Images" is the complete set of pictures in Document.

```
(picset=document.images);
```

The next step is called a Loop. The program is going to cycle, or loop, through the collection we just defined. Translated into English, the loop says "Start with zero. Count up by ones. Stop when you get to the number of pictures in picset. And at every count, do the bit of code within the brackets." Inside the brackets, we find the heart of our program. This is an IF statement that checks the current picture against our Banner Ad criteria.

```
for(n=0;n<picset.length;n++){if((picset[n].height==60)&&(picset[n].width=
➡=468))
```

Now, we need to indicate what should be done if an image meets the size specification. If the picture height is equal to 60 pixels, and the picture width is equal to 486, then take out the image and replace it with our custom one. Of course, the image we've specified in the following example doesn't actually exist. You need to point it to an image on your blog, favorite website, or even on your hard drive. Be sure to properly prepare the image you choose by making sure it is the correct size (486 X 60 pixels) and save it as a .gif file. Any image editor should be able to do this.

```
void(picset[n].src="http://www.yourbannerwebsite/yourbannerimage.gif");
```

It's time to close out the For Loop, so we need a closing bracket.

```
}
```

And we're ready to close out the entire function, so we need another closing bracket.

```
}
```

Now, name the function and complete the Anchor tag, and you're done.

```
NoBanner();'>No More Banner Ads Here!</A>
```

So, when you put it all together, it looks like this:

```
<A HREF='javascript:function%20NoBanner(){(picset=document.images);
for(n=0;n<picset.length;n++){if((picset[n].height==60)&&(picset[n].width=
➥=468)) void(picset[n].src="http://www.yourbannerwebsite/
➥yourbannerimage.gif");}}
NoBanner();'>No More Banner Ads Here!</A>
```

When you type this in, be sure to enter it in one long string, with no line breaks or spaces. Otherwise, you'll get an error message.

Now name the file, and save it to your desktop as a file with a .htm extension. If Chrome is your default browser, an icon that looks like the Chrome icon is created on your desktop. This new link has the same name as the file you just saved.

To install the bookmarklet, follow these steps:

1. Open Google Chrome.

2. Use the new desktop icon to open the file that contains the script we just created. It looks like Figure 10.8.

3. Drag the link to your Chrome Bookmarks bar.

Wasn't that easy?

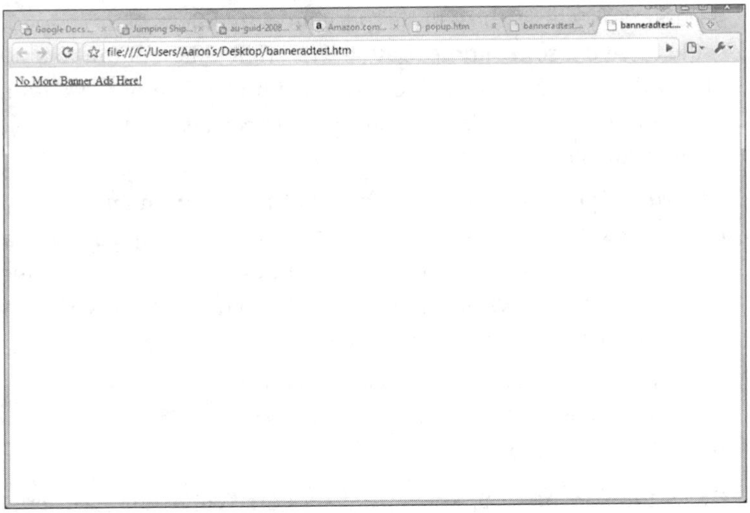

FIGURE 10.8
Your first bookmarklet!

And a Bit of Grease

Greasemonkey and Greasemetal scripts give a new versatility to Google Chrome. They both give Chrome users the ability to add functionality to Chrome. With a little imagination, the possibilities are endless. Like bookmarklets, Greasemonkey and Greasemetal scripts are written in JavaScript. Unlike bookmarkets, these scripts are not limited in the number of characters you can use.

In the following example, our script scans the web page you're surfing for inappropriate content, however you define it, by using a keyword search. If your keywords are found, the page auto redirects to a web page of your choice. For this test program, we redirect to none other than Google Geek.

Every Greasemonkey script starts with a UserScript block. This is a set of lines that describe the script to the Greasemonkey engine.

```
// ==UserScript==
```

Notice the // at the beginning of the line? This marks the line as a comment. When Greasemonkey runs the code, these lines are not included in the Javascript code, but the Greasemonkey program itself does look for them. The @name line is the name of the script.

```
// @name     Redirector
```

Greasemonkey uses the @namespace label to differentiate scripts. Two scripts could have the same names but be written by different authors with completely different functions. The URL listed under @namespace is one way to tell them apart. Most Greasemonkey script writers put the URL to their home page in this slot.

The @description line describes the script's function in English. You can leave this blank if you like, but it's helpful to put something here, because you might add a new script six months from now with the same name. The only way to tell the two scripts apart then is to go through the code, line by line, to figure out what each one really does.

```
// @namespace    http://www.google-geek.com/
// @description   Leap to a different web page if particular words are
➥found on this one.
```

Greasemonkey needs to know what sites are "valid" for each script. For example, you might want your script to run on the front page of somedomain.com, but not run on somedomain.com/detailspage.html. This is controlled by the @include and @exclude statements.

The @include and @exclude use the asterisk as a wild card, so http://google-geek.com/* matches any subdomain under the google-geek.com main domain. You need to specify both with and without the "www" on the front, if the website is valid under both. And @exclude trumps @include—meaning, if there is a disagreement between including and excluding something, the exclude wins. In our example code, this script is meant to run on all URLs because of the @include *, but it will not work on either of the Google Geek URLs, because they've been specifically excluded.

```
// @include     *
// @exclude     http://google-geek.com/*
// @exclude     http://www.google-geek.com/*
```

The order of the items in the UserScript block is not important, but it does have to have both start and end Userscript tags.

```
// ==/UserScript==
```

Javascript requires that all variable be "Declared" before they can be used, and we do this with the VAR command. Most of these variables are used within the program itself, but there's one that needs to be populated right now—the word list.

The following code declares the variables and tells Greasemonkey what to look for in the page text. Enter your search criteria between the quotes, in the wordList string. Separate the words with commas, but do not add a space between words. Choose your words carefully, because if any of these words exist on the website you visit, the browser will immediately jump to another site.

```
var wordList, wordArray, bodyText, n, snip, z, findit, foundit;
wordList="Enter,search,words,here,separated,by,commas"
```

Next, change the list into an array, so Greasemonkey can search for each word in turn. Javascript will have a much easier time searching an array rather than a list of words. The Split command breaks up the Wordlist by creating a new record in the array every time it finds a comma.

```
wordArray=wordList.split(",")
```

Now, load the page text into the program so it can be checked for the flagged words. This chunk of code is an XPath command. XPath is a Javascript command that collects data from a web page. For this particular command, XPath is going to gather up all of the text entries of the website our browser is viewing, and it's going to store them in the variable bodyText.

```
bodyText = document.evaluate(
  "//text()",
  document,
  null,
  XPathResult.UNORDERED_NODE_SNAPSHOT_TYPE,
  null);
```

It's time to loop through the text. Our loop starts counting at zero (n=0). At every step through the loop, it increments, or adds one, to our counter (n++). It will keep counting until it reaches bodyshot.snapshotLength—that is, until it counts once for every record in the bodyText variable. And at each step, take the existing text item, and store it in the variable snip.

```
for (n = 0; n < bodyText.snapshotLength; n++)
  snip = bodyText.snapshotItem(n); {
```

We need a second loop here. For every text item, we need to cycle through all of the entries in our word list. We could do the same kind of loop we used above, but since we know how many entries there are in our list, we can use a shorter version of the for/next structure. For (z in wordArray) cycles through every entry in our wordArray variable. We'll store whatever that word is in findIt, and then use snip.search to check if that word exists in our website text. If there is a match, the variable, foundIt, changes.

```
for (z in wordArray) {
findIt = /wordArray[z]/gi;
foundIt = snip.search(findit)
```

And, finally, if a word in the text matches a word in the flagged list—that is, if there's anything stored in foundIt—redirect to www.google-geek.com.

```
if (foundIt >0)
```

```
window.location.href = 'http://www.google-geek.com/'
```

Remember to close all the brackets; otherwise, it won't run.

```
} //closes the inner (wordArray) loop
} //closes the outer (snip) loop
```

Name and save to C:\Scripts. Make sure you save as a .js or JavaScript file. If Chrome is open, restart it to run the script.

Closing the Door

Now that you have a basic understanding of how to build themes, bookmarklets, and Greasemonkey scripts, the only thing left to add is your own imagination. Next, in Chapter 11, we'll look at some interesting and powerful hacks you can use to extend Chrome's functionality. These hacks represent some of the most advanced capabilities of Chrome.

Chrome for Power Users

In this part:

- Chrome Hacks for the Power User
- Troubleshooting Google Chrome

Even though this is the shortest part of the book, don't let it fool you. This part contains plenty of information to help you really get the most out of Chrome. The power users chapter provides some deep customization tricks that you can use to really make Chrome work for you.

Of course, even the best designed applications occasionally have issues, so the troubleshooting chapter helps if you happen to run into problems. Don't worry, there aren't a whole lot of problems to encounter, and we cover the most common ones.

Once you're through these two chapters, you should know just about all there is to know about Google Chrome. So, what are you waiting for? Go after it.

Chrome Hacks for the Power Users

By all outward appearances, Google Chrome looks deceptively simple. Truth is, though the user interface is simple, there's far more power inside Google Chrome than you may have realized when you first picked up this book.

This far into it, though, you should not be surprised that there's more you can do with Chrome than meets the eye. In this chapter, you learn some of the most advanced capabilities of Chrome. Some of them everyone will use; others are neat tricks that are really only of value to developers or the most advanced web users.

Skim through the chapter and pick and choose what you need. Just remember, you can always refer back to the chapter as your skills and the number of tasks you complete with Chrome increase.

Skinning Google Chrome

One of the most frequently heard complaints about Chrome when it was first released was that there were no themes or appearance customization options for the browser. Other than being able to add or remove a toolbar here and there, you were pretty much stuck with the way that Chrome looked, even if it was dead boring.

Well, you were stuck with it for about two seconds. One of the first Chrome hacks released was how to add different themes to your browser. It's not too difficult to do, but you are going to have to monkey around with the code just a bit.

Before you can even begin to change the theme on your browser, you need to find a theme you like. You can do that by performing a quick Google search for "Google Chrome themes." Navigate through the search results until you find something you like, and then download it, making note of where the file downloads to, because you need to get to it later.

11

Once you have the theme that you want to use, you need to unzip that file. When you unzip the file, note where it's unzipping to, as you need access to those files. If your unzip utility automatically opens the file when it's finished decompressing the zip file, you can just leave that window open temporarily.

Once your theme is downloaded and unzipped, you can begin the process of installing the new theme on your Chrome browser, using these steps:

1. Themes in Chrome are changed by changing the default.dll file. Before you change this file, however, you need to find it. Make sure Chrome is closed, and then open the **Run** dialog box (in Windows XP go to the **Start** menu and select **Run**, in Windows Vista just type the following command into the Start menu box). Then type the following string in the Run dialog box and press **Enter** (as shown in Figure 11.1):

```
local settings\Application Data\Google\Chrome\Application
```

FIGURE 11.1
Run the location string to access Google Chrome files used to change Chrome themes.

If you're using Windows Vista you can also type appdata into the **Run** dialog box (which is actually the **Start** menu search box) and then press **Enter**. When the app-data files appear, navigate to local\Google\Chrome\Application.

2. The folder in which the Chrome files are stored opens, as shown in Figure 11.2. Double-click on the folder name that's made up of numbers such as **1.0.154.48** (the number might be different for the Chrome version that you're running) to open it.

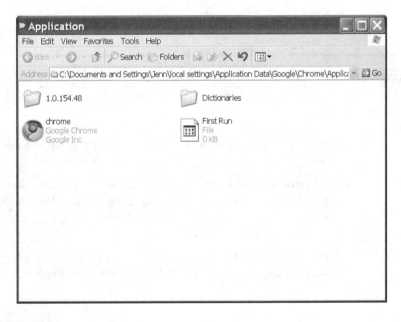

FIGURE 11.2
All the Chrome files are stored in this single location. You need to access the file named by a number string.

3. Double-click the **Themes** folder, shown in Figure 11.3. When the folder opens, there should be a single item: default.dll. Before you go any further, right-click that file and select **Copy**; then minimize your windows until you can see your desktop. Right-click the desktop and select **Paste**. Now, you have a backup copy of the original .dll file should you need to revert back to the default theme for Chrome.

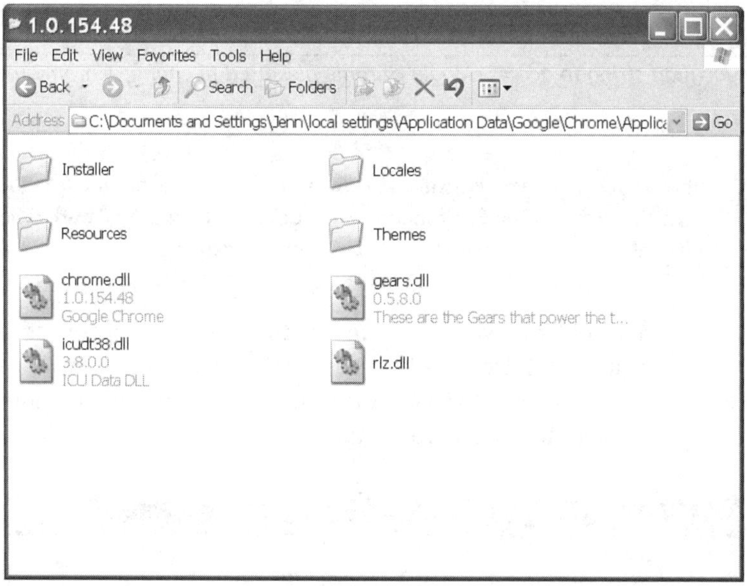

FIGURE 11.3

The default.dll file is located in the Themes folder. This single file controls the theme of your Chrome browser.

4. After you've made a copy of the default.dll file, delete the one in the **Themes** folder.

5. Now, remember when you unzipped the theme you downloaded? Open that folder and you should find a file there labeled default.dll. Copy that file and paste it into the **Themes** folder (where you deleted the other default.dll a short while ago).

6. Close all the open windows and open your Chrome browser. The new theme should take the place of the default Chrome theme.

The whole process looks a little harder than it is. Once you run through it the first time, you'll find that it takes less than a minute to change default.dll files whenever you feel like you need a new theme for Chrome.

No Joke Be aware of two cautions for changing the theme of your Chrome browser. First, some themes won't work with the version of the browser that you have. You may have to try several different themes before you find one that works.

The second thing for you to be aware of is malware. Not every theme that you find is necessarily created by a legitimate developer. Some may be created by hackers and other criminals. We suggest that you only download themes from websites that you trust and always look at reviews of the theme before you actually download the file.

Taking Control with Bookmarks

Another problem that some users have with Chrome is that they miss the widgets and add-ons that you can get with some other browsers. Personally, I love the ability to click a single link on my Bookmarks bar, perform a task, and never have to leave the page that I'm on. I also like having the ability to single-click to go to a favorite web page. And that's where Chrome really works for you. So, how do you combine the two?

It starts by wanting the Chrome Bookmarks bar to be bigger. I love the Bookmarks bar. It's one of the most used features of Chrome for me, but you can only have eight or so bookmarks on the Bookmarks bar. Or you could in the past....

Increase the Capacity of the Bookmarks Bar

There's another way to extend the availability of bookmark real estate on the Bookmarks bar. You can make it display icons only:

1. From the open Google Chrome browser, right-click any bookmark on the Bookmarks bar and select **Edit**, as shown in Figure 11.4.

2. The **Edit Bookmark** dialog box appears, as shown in Figure 11.5. Highlight the name of the bookmark and then delete it. That leaves the **Name** box on the Edit window blank.

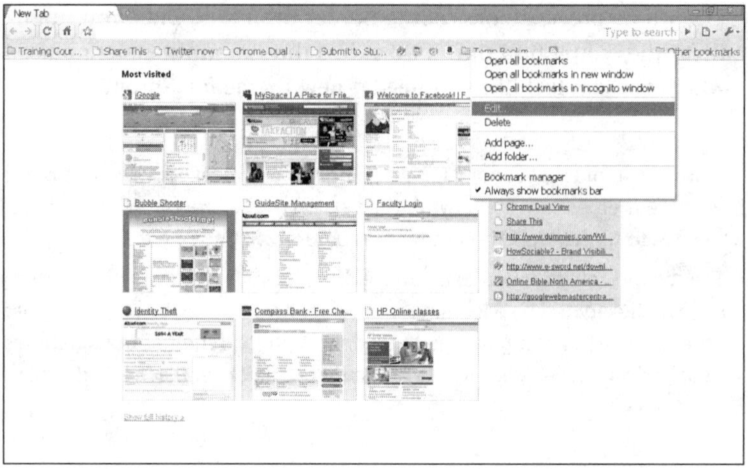

FIGURE 11.4

Select Edit to open a window that allows you to change information about the selected bookmark.

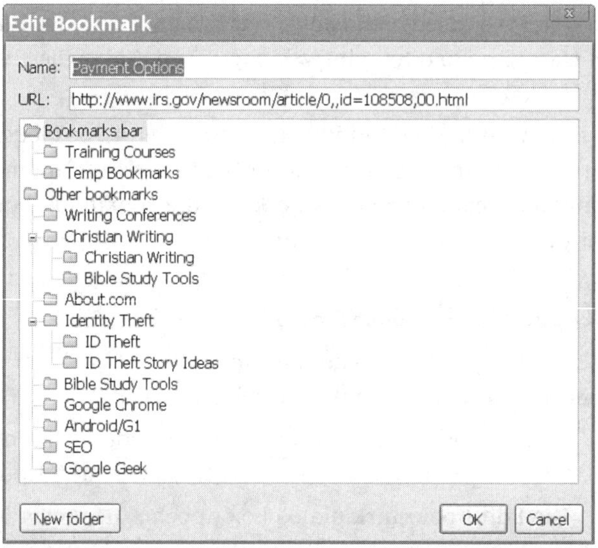

FIGURE 11.5

Use the Edit Bookmark dialog box to change features of a bookmark such as the name or the URL.

3. Click **OK**. What's left on the Bookmarks bar is just the icon for the link. You can repeat that with all the bookmarks on the Bookmarks bar to open up real estate. As shown in Figure 11.6, when just the icons are showing, you can add many more bookmarks to the Bookmarks bar.

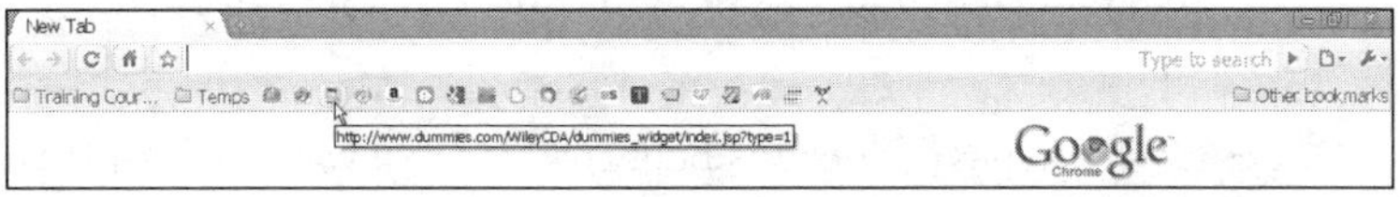

FIGURE 11.6

By showing only the icons for the pages you want to access from the Bookmarks bar, you can add many more sites to the bar.

One more thing about the icons that you see in the Bookmarks bar: if you've imported bookmarks from another web browser, your imported bookmarks will appear with generic icons until you visit the site. It's not until you've actually gone to a bookmark that Chrome can collect the icon information needed to replace the generic icon. So, if you're just getting started, you might want to visit all of your bookmarked pages before you begin changing the appearance of the bookmark icons.

Changing Bookmark Icons

One thing you may notice as you're going through your bookmarks is that many bookmarks don't have icons. Bookmarks without icons have a simple folder designation (for folders of bookmarks) or a page icon.

Now, the whole concept of reducing your Bookmarks bar to icons is great, unless you have multiple pages that show up with the page icon. Then how are you supposed to know (at a glance) what the link is? Of course, you can hover over the link (refer to Figure 11.6) to see the URL, but that defeats the purpose of glance-and-click, doesn't it?

You can solve that problem if you have a little time and the desire. All you have to do is create icons for your bookmarks that you'll recognize. Here's how:

1. Before you begin, you need to download and install the SQLite Database browser. You can download this file from the SourceForge website using this URL: http://sourceforge.net/project/showfiles. php?group_id=87946.

2. After you've completed the installation of the SQLite Database browser, open Google Chrome and visit the websites that have icons that you want to display on your Bookmarks bar. This process might take you some time to complete, especially if you're not sure where those icons are located. When you're done, close Google Chrome.

Yellow Box Icons for web pages can be just about anything that you want them to be, however, pages that have clearly understood logos are usually best. For example, if you're trying to find an icon for Google Docs (specifically) you might not want the standard Google icon that appears on most Google bookmarks. Instead, you can navigate to a page that has a better document icon and then use that instead. The best way to locate icons you might want to use is to search for pages like the one that you have bookmarked.

3. Open the SQLite Database browser. Once it's open, click the **Open** icon (or select **File, Open Database** or press **Ctrl+O**).

4. The **Open** dialog box appears. Navigate to the following directory (making sure to change the "username" portion of the path to your computer username):

In Windows XP:

C:\Documents and Settings\username\Local Settings\Application Data\Google\Chrome\User Data\Default

In Windows Vista:

C:\Users\username\AppData\Local\Google\Chrome\User Data\Default

5. From the dialog box that appears (shown in Figure 11.7), open the History file.

6. Select the **Browse Data** tab, and a list of URLs appears, as shown in Figure 11.8.

7. Now, you need to change the way the data is sorted, so from the **Table** drop-down menu, select **urls**. When the data refreshes, the table appears with the following columns: **id**, **url**, **title**, **visit_count**, **typed_count**, **last_visit_time**, **hidden**, **favicon_id**, and **starred_id**.

Mainly, we're interested in the **favicon_id** column because this is where we find the image information that we need, but we also need to refer to the **title** column to find the websites that have the icons for which you're looking. Any row that has a value other than 0 in the **favicon_id** column has an icon associated with it (if it has a 0, it uses the default icon).

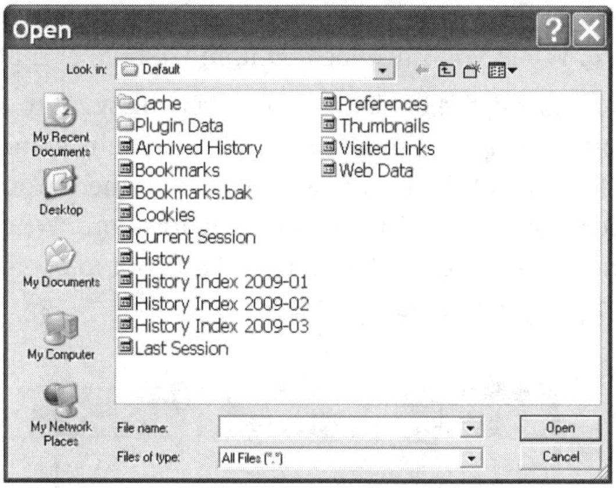

FIGURE 11.7

Use the dialog box to navigate into the History folder (not the History Index XX folder).

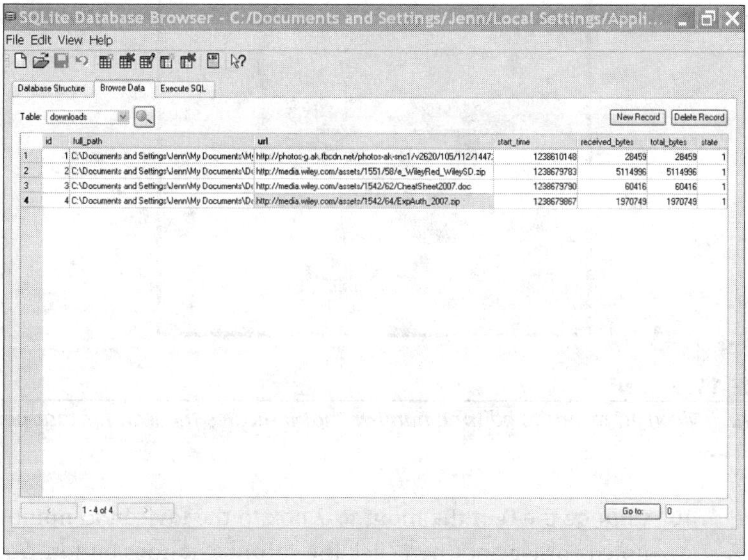

FIGURE 11.8

There is a list of all the URLs that you have browsed. If the list is too long, you can clear your browser cache and start again for a shorter list.

8. Locate one of the sites you browsed to earlier that contains the desired icon that you want to use. It could take you a while to find it, depending on the number of records that are there, but usually you'll find a group of sites that are related once you find the first one. This is important because you need to have the **favicon_id** value from a related site. When you have located it, make note of that value.

9. Now locate the bookmark to which you want to assign the icon. The title may appear more than once, so you need to repeat this process with each of the instances that appear there. You're looking for related sites that have a **0** in the **favicon_id** record. When you find one of these, double-click the **favicon_id** record to open a dialog box like the one shown in Figure 11.9.

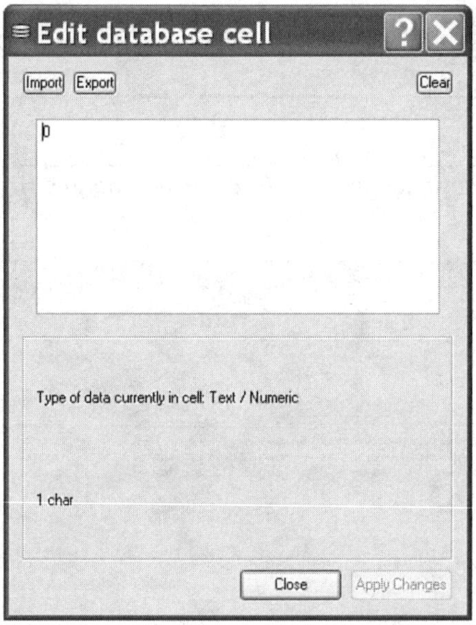

FIGURE 11.9

Open the favicon_id record to edit the number that indicates the icon for that particular website.

10. Change the 0 in the main text box to the favicon id number that you noted earlier and then click the **Apply Changes** button. You are returned to the database browser.

11. Repeat this process until you have finished assigning icons to your bookmarks and then go to **File, Save Database** (or just click the **Save** icon on the database browser toolbar); then close the database browser.

12. The next time that you open Google Chrome, all the links in your Bookmarks bar should reflect the changes that you made, making it easier for you to spot the bookmark for which you're looking.

Adding Bookmarklets

Of course, icons aren't the only cool trick that you can manage with your Bookmarks bar. As you learned in Chapter 9, "Spit-Shining Chrome," you can also install *bookmarklets* that allow you to quickly access applications and programs that are much like the widgets that you probably used with other browsers. For example, one bookmarklet allows you to post directly to your Twitter account from whatever website you happen to be visiting.

geek speak

Bookmarklets are mini-applications that you can run from your bookmarks. These work like gadgets or widgets; they're small applications with a bit of functionality used by the whole program they represent. So, for example, the Twitter bookmarklet allows you to send tweets from whatever page you happen to be surfing on. You don't have to log in to or navigate to the application to take advantage of some of the most used features.

11

In Chapter 9, the bookmarklets covered were largely drag-and-drop—you navigate to a website and then drag and drop a link to your Bookmarks bar to add the bookmarklet to the bar. There's another way to create a bookmarklet, too, and it isn't difficult at all. All you have to do is create a new bookmark and instead of using a URL, you add in the code that executes the action you want to have happen. Of course, you'll have to write the bookmarklet code for the desired action unless someone else provides it for you. Then it's as easy as creating a new bookmark. These steps should make it clearer:

1. From within the Chrome browser, right-click on the **Bookmarks bar** and select **Add page**.

2. The **Edit Bookmark** dialog appears, as shown in Figure 11.10.

3. Enter the name of the bookmarklet you want to create in the **Name** text box.

4. Paste (or enter) the code for the bookmarklet into the **URL** box.

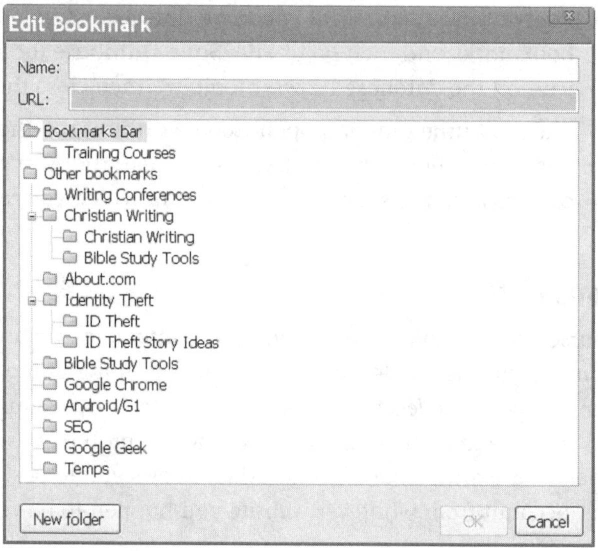

FIGURE 11.10
Use the Edit Bookmark dialog to change an existing bookmark or create a new one.

5. Make sure that **Bookmarks Bar** is selected as the folder you want the bookmarklet to appear in, and then click **OK**.

6. The Edit Bookmark dialog closes, and you're taken back to Chrome, but you should see the bookmarklet appear on the Bookmarks bar. (Bookmarklets are usually indicated by a generic page icon, so be sure you follow the naming step.)

That's easy enough, right? But where do you get the code for the bookmarklets? If you're not inclined to program the bookmarklet yourself, you can find plenty of places on the Web where bookmarklets and bookmarklet code are available.

Still, we don't want to introduce a new skill and not give you the opportunity to use it, so the following sections present a few examples of the bookmarklet code that you might find on the Web.

No Joke The code for the bookmarklets detailed in the following sections is to create bookmarks for applications or services to which you must subscribe. You'll need to have an account to these services to be able to properly use the bookmarklets for them, once the bookmarklets have been created.

Delicious Bookmarklet

```
javascript:(function()%7bf='http://delicious.com/save?url='+encodeURI
➥Component(window.location.href)+'&title='+encodeURIComponent
➥(document.title)+'&v=5&';a=function()%7bif(!window.open(f+'noui=1&jump=
➥doclose','deliciousuiv5','location=yes,links=no,scrollbars=no,toolbar=
➥no,width=550,height=550'))location.href=f+'jump=yes'%7d;if(/Firefox/
➥.test(navigator.userAgent))%7bsetTimeout(a,0)%7delse%7ba()%7d%7d)()
```

The Delicious bookmarklet works for people who have a del.icio.us account. Using this bookmarklet, you can add any page on which you're surfing to your del.icio.us bookmarks just by clicking the bookmark. When you do, a dialog box opens, prompting you to sign into your account. Once you're signed in, the bookmark is added to your account.

Twitter Bookmarklet

```
javascript:s1=new%20String('http://twittercard.com/tinyurl.php?t='+encode
➥URIComponent(document.title)+'&u='+encodeURIComponent(document.
➥location.href));void(window.open(s1));
```

Twitter is another social media application that many people use to share information that they find on the web. Using this bookmarklet, you can post a link to your Twitter feed to any web page and you can do it directly from the bookmarklets bar.

StumbleUpon Bookmarklet

```
javascript:document.location.href='http://www.stumbleupon.com/submit?url=
➥'+document.URL+'&title='+document.title.replace(/%20/g,'+');
```

Use the StumbleUpon bookmarklet to add web pages that you find interesting to the StumbleUpon directory. Once you've created this bookmarklet, select it when you're on any page on the Web that you want to share via the StumbleUpon service. You're then taken to the StumbleUpon rate and review page where you can rate the page and give it your personal review. When you're finished, however, you'll have to navigate back to the page that you rated.

11

FriendFeed Bookmarklet

```
javascript:void((function()%7bvar%20e=document.createElement('script');
e.setAttribute('type','text/javascript');e.setAttribute('src','http://
friendfeed.com/share/bookmarklet/javascript');document.body.appendChild
(e)%7d)())
```

The FriendFeed bookmarklet works like the others that you've seen already. Simply add the bookmarklet to your bookmarks bar, and then click it when you find something that you want to share through your FriendFeed. A small popup window appears in the right corner of the web page where you can enter the group you want to share it with and add any comments that you might like to include. Click **Post** when you're done to send the feed.

TinyURL Bookmarklet

```
javascript:void(window.open('http://tinyurl.com/create.php?url='+
document.location.href));
```

Ever find a website that you want to share with others, but the URL wraps for more than one line? Like this:

```
http://www.amazon.com/SEO-Search-Engine-Optimization-Bible/dp/0470452641/
ref=pd_bbs_sr_1?ie=UTF8&s=books&qid=1238690231&sr=8-1
```

When a URL wraps like that, it can perform poorly when someone clicks on it. In other words, the link might not work if it wraps. But using the TinyURL bookmarklet, you can change that URL into one that's much shorter. Like this:

http://tinyurl.com/d7er9r

All you need to do is create the bookmarklet, then when you're on a page that you want to share with others, click the bookmark. You're taken to a TinyURL web page (a separate tab, actually) where the URL has been converted to the shorter, TinyURL version that you can share with your friends.

ShareThis Bookmarklet

```
javascript:var%20e=document.createElement('script');e.setAttribute
('language','javascript');e.setAttribute('src','http://sharethis.com/
share/load');document.body.appendChild(e);void(0);
```

ShareThis is the mother of all social bookmarking services. Rather than being a separate service, ShareThis is a service that aggregates all of your social bookmarking options into one place. Then, when you find something online that you want to share with other members of your social network—whether it's Twitter, Facebook, MySpace, del.icio.us, Blogger, Reddit, or one of more than a dozen others—all you have to do is click the bookmarklet.

Once you've created this bookmarklet and you find something online you want to share, just click the bookmarklet, choose the service that you want to share it with, and then follow the prompts for sharing through that service. This is perhaps one of the most useful bookmarklets included here if you're a social media user because it's nice to have all of those services available from a single button on your Bookmarks bar.

Print from the Bookmarks Bar

One last bit of coolness for the Bookmarks bar that you might appreciate is the ability to put a Print button on that bar. Printing from Chrome can be accomplished in two ways. You can either use the keyboard shortcut (**Ctrl+P**) or you can go to the page controls menu and select **Print**. But wouldn't it be easier just to click an icon on the Bookmarks bar?

Here's how it's done:

1. From within Chrome, right-click on an empty space on the Bookmarks bar and select **Add page**.

2. The **Edit Bookmark** dialog that you worked with earlier in this chapter (refer to Figure 11.10) appears. In the **Name** text box, enter the name Print.

3. In the **URL** text box, enter the following snippet of code: javascript:window.print() and then make sure the **Bookmarks Bar** folder is selected.

4. Click **OK**. You are returned to the browser, where a **Print** icon now appears on the Bookmarks bar. The icon is the generic page icon, but when you click it the Print dialog box opens, as shown in Figure 11.11.

11

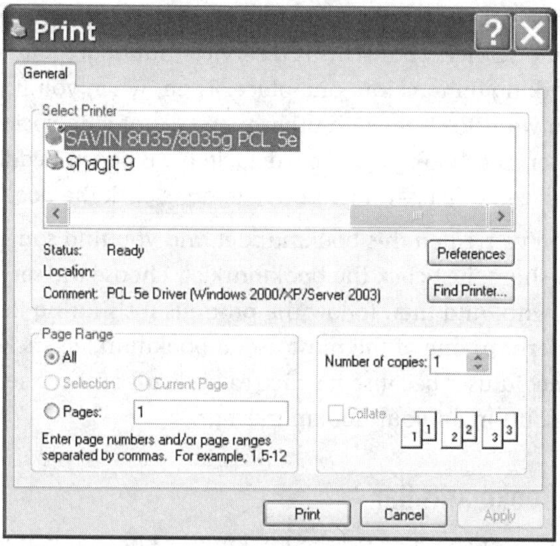

FIGURE 11.11
Once you place a print bookmarklet on the Bookmarks bar, printing is as simple as point-and-click.

Creating Profiles in Google Chrome

One problem that you might encounter as you make the move to Google Chrome is that it doesn't inherently have multiple profiles. So, if you're using the same computer that other people are using, you may not have the privacy that you would like to have.

Fortunately, other Chrome users experienced the same problem and came up with a couple of ways to manually create multiple profiles or profiles for different purposes. Let's start with multiple profiles.

Creating Multiple User Profiles in Chrome

It would have been nice if the capability for multiple user profiles had been built in to Chrome. Unfortunately, the closest that you get to multiple user profiles in Chrome is the Incognito mode that you can access when you don't want someone following your surfing movements.

Well, that was the closest you could get until someone figured out how to create multiple user profiles. Here are the steps you can use to do it too:

1. Open Google Chrome and open the **Tools** menu (to the right of the Omnibox). In the menu that appears, select **Clear Browsing Data**.

2. In the dialog box that appears (shown in Figure 11.12), select the **Clear Data from This Period** drop-down menu and choose the **Everything** option. This clears all the browsing history in Chrome. The browsing history needs to be cleared to enable the different profiles that you create.

No Joke   Be aware! When you select to clear everything in your browsing history, you're literally going to lose everything that's not deselected in the **Obliterate the Following Items** list. That includes the pages that appear on your new tab as well as usernames and passwords if the option is checked. Be sure that any information that you might need to keep is deselected before you choose to clear everything.

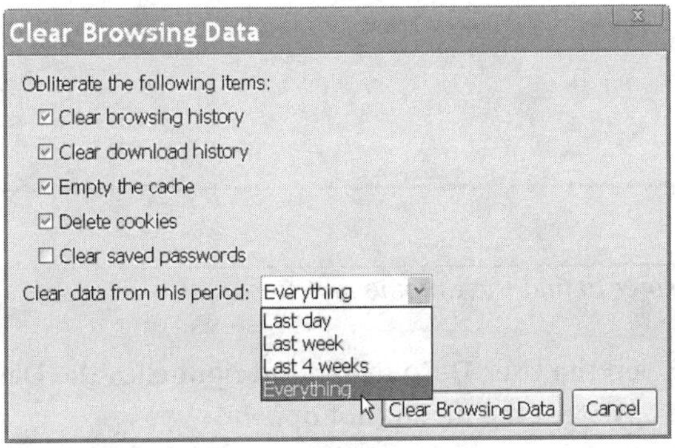

Clear Browsing Data

Obliterate the following items:

☑ Clear browsing history
☑ Clear download history
☑ Empty the cache
☑ Delete cookies
☐ Clear saved passwords

Clear data from this period: Everything

Last day
Last week
Last 4 weeks
Everything

Clear Browsing Data   Cancel

FIGURE 11.12

Clear your Internet history and cache in the Clear Browsing Data dialog box. You can select types of data to be cleared or deselect them to keep the data.

3. Now you need to open the Chrome installation folder that we worked with earlier in this chapter. You'll find those here:

In Windows XP:

C:\Documents and Settings\username\Local Settings\Application Data\Google\Chrome\Application

In Windows Vista:

C:\Users\username\AppData\Local\Google\Chrome\Application

4. Open the address bar of the Windows Explorer, as shown in Figure 11.13 and select the **Chrome** folder.

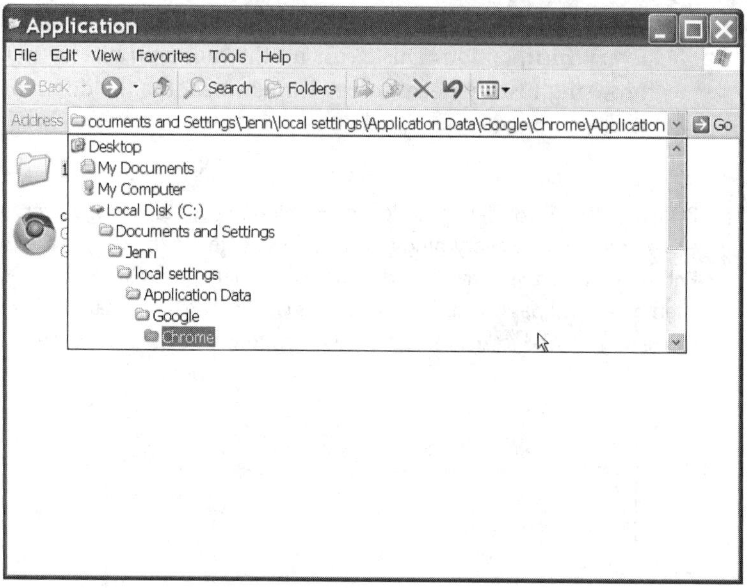

FIGURE 11.13

Use Windows Explorer to find the Chrome folder.

5. Open the **User Data** folder and right-click the **Default** folder. Select **Copy** from the menu that appears.

6. Now, paste that copied folder *in the same file*, but change the name to **Your_Name**, as shown in Figure 11.14. (Note that you can actually name the file whatever you want; this is just for demonstration purposes.)

7. Now, you need to initialize the new profile. To do that, open Chrome and type the following string into the Omnibox; then press **Enter** (remember to replace "Your_Name" with the name that you used when you created the new profile):

```
chrome.exe —user-data-dir="..\User Data\Your_Name" -first-run
```

After you press **Enter**, the new Chrome profile loads in place of the previous profile you were using.

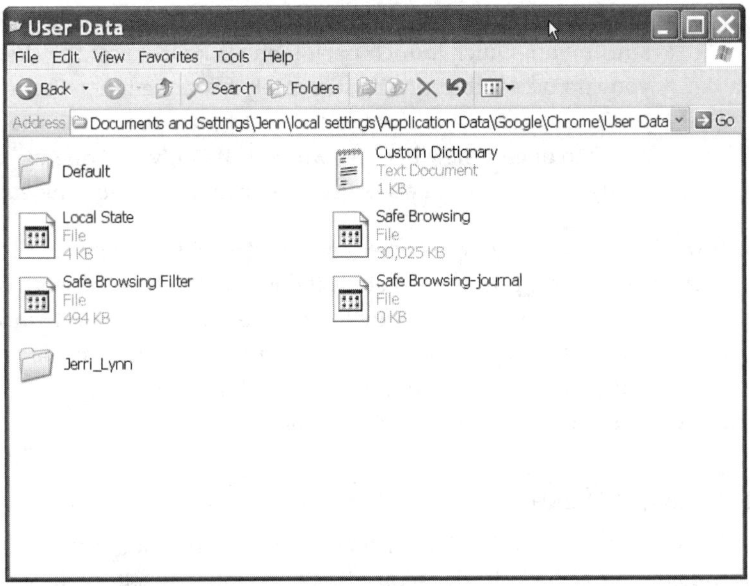

User Data window showing:

- Default
- Local State — File 4 KB
- Safe Browsing Filter — File 494 KB
- Jerri_Lynn
- Custom Dictionary — Text Document 1 KB
- Safe Browsing — File 30,025 KB
- Safe Browsing-journal — File 0 KB

Address: Documents and Settings\Jenn\local settings\Application Data\Google\Chrome\User Data

FIGURE 11.14

Copy the new folder into the same file, but be sure to change the name of the new folder.

8. Finally, you need to create a shortcut to this new Chrome profile. Do that while you have the new Chrome profile open. Click the page controls icon and select **Create Application Shortcuts**. A new Google Gears dialog box opens, as shown in Figure 11.15.

Google Gears dialog box:

chrome.exe --user-data-dir=_.._User Data_Jerri_Lynn_ -first-run

Create shortcuts in the following locations:

- ☑ Desktop
- ☐ Start menu
- ☐ Quick launch bar

[OK] [Cancel]

FIGURE 11.15

Google Gears are part of what makes it possible for you to create shortcuts to applications through the Chrome browser.

9. Just select how and where you want the shortcut to appear (Desktop, Start menu, Quick launch bar); then click **OK** to set the shortcut. Now you can access that profile separately from the other Chrome profile. Just double-click the Chrome shortcut that you want to use when you're ready to open a new browser window. If you've set one up to use separately from everyone else's then you can access that one each time.

It would be really nice if Chrome gave you the ability to set up the browser with different user profiles, but since it doesn't, you have to work around the problem. This solution is one way to create a separate Chrome profile for another user on your computer. And if you truly don't want the other user on your profile, consider changing the icon and the name that you display to something only you recognize as your browser.

Command-Line Switches

Having separate profiles for Chrome users is pretty cool. It lets you set up something for the kids, the spouse, visitors, and yourself—you can also have multiple personal accounts if that's what you really want. But you can also further tweak those profiles by using *command-line switches.*

geek speak   *Command-line switches* are parameters that can be added to the command line when starting Chrome that make it behave slightly differently than if the command-line switches were not there. These switches enable or disable functionality such as Java, images, and metrics reporting.

A command-line switch can be used for nearly 75 different functions in Chrome. You can speed up browsing by disabling functions, and you can even block various plug-ins, features, and content that you don't like.

To use a startup switch, follow these steps:

1. Create a new Chrome shortcut on your desktop and then right-click it.

2. In the menu that appears, select **Properties**. This opens the **Properties** dialog box, shown in Figure 11.16.

3. In the Properties dialog box, in the **Target** field, append the switch code you want to use to the end of the path to chrome.exe. Be sure to include a space between the end of the .exe command and the command-line switch code. For example, your target using a -disable-java switch might look like this:

```
"C:\Documents and Settings\gina\Local Settings\ApplicationData\
➥Google\Chrome\Application\chrome.exe " -disable-java
```

4. Once you add the command-line switch to the .exe command, click **Apply** and **OK** to save the changes. The next time you open Chrome, the command-line switch is activated.

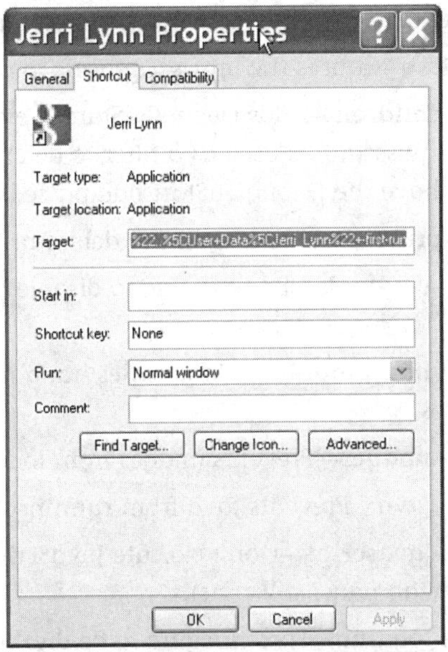

FIGURE 11.16
Use the Properties dialog box to add a command-line switch to Chrome.

A variety of different command-line switches are available for you to use. A list of some of the Chrome startup switches that are available include

- **allow-all-activex**—Allow initialization of all ActiveX controls. This is only to help website developers test their controls to see if they are compatible in Chrome. Note that there is a duplicate value in ActiveX: *shared.cc* (to avoid dependency on chrome module). Make sure you change both locations at the same time.

- **always-enable-dev-tools**—Enable web inspector for all windows, even if they're part of the browser. Allows developers to use dev tools to debug the browser window.

- **app**—Specifies that the associated value should be launched in "application" mode.

- **assert-test**—Causes the browser process to throw an assertion on startup.

- **automation-channel**—The value of this switch tells the app to listen for and broadcast automation-related messages on IPC channel with the given ID.

- **channel**—The value of this switch tells the child process which IPC channel the browser expects to use to communicate with it.

- **crash-test**—Causes the browser process to crash on startup.

- **debug-children**—Adds DebugOnStart to every child processes. If a value is passed, it is used as a filter to determine if the child process should have the DebugOnStart flag passed on or not.

- **debug-print**—Enables support to debug printing subsystem.

- **disable-dev-tools**—Browser flag to disable the web inspector for all renderers.

- **disable-hang-monitor**—Suppresses hang monitor dialogs in renderer processes.

- **disable-images**—Prevents images from loading.

- **disable-java**—Prevents Java from running.

- **disable-javascript**—Don't execute JavaScript (browser JavaScript, like the new tab page, still runs).

- **disable-logging**—Force logging to be disabled. Logging is enabled by default in debug builds.

- **disable-metrics**—Completely disables UMA metrics system.

- **disable-metrics-reporting**—Disables only the sending of metrics reports. In contrast to DisableMetrics, this executes all the code that a normal client would use for reporting, except the report is dropped rather than sent to the server. This is useful for finding issues in the metrics code during UI and performance tests.

- **disable-plugins**—Prevent plugins from running.

- **disable-popup-blocking**—Disable pop-up blocking.

- **disable-prompt-on-repost**—Normally when the user attempts to navigate to a page that was the result of a post we prompt to make sure that is what they want to do. Use this switch to disable that check. This switch is used during automated testing.

- **dns-log-details**—Chrome supports pre-fetching of DNS information. This information is then stored in a log file.

- **dns-prefetch-disable**—Chrome supports pre-fetching of DNS information by default. You can use this switch to disable this functionality.

- **dom-automation**—Specifies if the dom_automation_controller_needs to be bound in the renderer. This binding happens on per-frame basis and hence can potentially be a performance bottleneck. You should only enable it when automating dom based tests.

- **dump-histograms-on-exit**—Dump any accumulated histograms to the log when the browser terminates (requires logging to be enabled to really do anything). Developers and test scripts most commonly use this switch.

- **enable-file-cookies**—By default, cookies are not allowed on file://. They are needed for testing, for example page cycler and layout tests.

- **enable-logging**—Force logging to be enabled. Logging is disabled by default in release builds.

- **enable-watchdog**—Spawn threads to watch for excessive delays in specified message loops. Users should set breakpoints on Alarm() to examine a problematic thread. Usage: -enable-watchdog=[ui][io]. Note that the order of the listed sub-arguments does not matter.

- **first-run**—Display the First Run experience when the browser is started, regardless of whether or not it's actually the first run.

- **geoid**—The GeoID developers should use. This is normally obtained from the operating system during first run and cached in the preferences afterwards. This is a numeric value. For more information, see http://msdn.microsoft.com/en-us/library/ms776390.aspx.

- **gears-in-renderer**—Switch to load Gears in the renderer process.

- **gears-plugin-path**—Debug only switch to specify which gears plug-in dll to load.

- **hide-icons**—Make Windows happy by allowing it to show "Enable access to this program" checkbox in Add/Remove Programs>Set Program Access and Defaults. This only shows an error box because the only way to hide Chrome is by uninstalling it.

- **homepage**—The value of this switch specifies which page will be displayed in newly opened tabs. This is for testing purposes so that the user interface tests don't depend on what comes up for http://google.com.

11

- **import**—Perform importing from another browser. The value associated with this setting encodes the target browser and what items to import.
- **in-process-plugins**—Runs plugins inside the renderer process.
- **javascript-debugger-path**—Allows loading of the JavaScript debugger user interface from the file system.
- **js-flags**—Specifies the flags passed to JS engine.
- **lang**—The language file that we want to try to open. Of the form language[-country] where language is the 2 letter code from ISO-639.
- **log-filter-prefix**—Filters log messages to show only the messages that are prefixed with the specified value.
- **log-level**—Sets the minimum log level. Valid values are from 0 to 3: INFO = 0, WARNING = 1, LOG_ERROR = 2, LOG_FATAL = 3.
- **make-default-browser**—Make Chrome the default browser.
- **memory-model**—Configure Chrome's memory model. Does Chrome really need multiple memory models? No. But this allows developers to experiment with a few choices.
- **memory-profile**—Enable dynamic loading of the Memory Profiler DLL, which traces all memory allocations during the run.
- **message-loop-histogrammer**—Enable histograming of tasks served by MessageLoop. See about:histograms/Loop for results, which shows frequency of messages on each thread, including APC count, object signaling count, and so on.
- **new-http**—Enable new HTTP stack.
- **no-events**—Don't record/playback events when using record & playback.
- **no-sandbox**—Runs the renderer outside the sandbox.
- **omnibox-popup-count**—Number of entries to show in the Omnibox popup.
- **playback-mode**—Chrome supports a playback and record mode. Playback mode reads data exclusively from the cache. This allows developers to record a session into the cache and then replay it at will.
- **plugin**—Causes the process to run as plugin host.
- **plugin-launcher**—Specifies a command that should be used to launch the plugin process. Useful for running the plugin process through purify or quantify. For example, plugin-launcher="path\to\purify /Run=yes".

- **plugin-path**—Tells the plug-in process the path of the plug-in to load.
- **plugin-startup-dialog**—Causes the plug-in process to display a dialog on launch.
- **process-per-site**—Runs a single process for each site (i.e., group of pages from the same registered domain) the user visits. Developers default to using a renderer process for each site instance (i.e., group of pages from the same registered domain with script connections to each other).
- **process-per-tab**—Runs each set of script-connected tabs (i.e., a BrowsingInstance) in its own renderer process. Developers default to using a renderer process for each site instance (i.e., group of pages from the same registered domain with script connections to each other).
- **proxy-server**—Use a specified proxy server, overrides system settings. This switch only affects HTTP and HTTPS requests.
- **upload-file**—Specifies the file that should be uploaded to the provided application. This switch is expected to be used with the --app option.
- **record-mode**—Chrome supports a playback and record mode. Record mode saves *everything* to the cache. This allows developers to record a session into the cache and then replay it at will.
- **remote-shell-port**—Enables remote debug/automation shell on the specified port.
- **renderer**—Causes the process to run as renderer instead of as browser.
- **renderer-assert-test**—Causes the renderer process to throw an assertion on launch.
- **renderer-crash-test**—Causes the renderer process to crash on launch.
- **renderer-path**—Path to the exe to run for the renderer subprocess.
- **renderer-startup-dialog**—Causes the renderer process to display a dialog on launch.
- **restore-last-session**—Indicates the last session should be restored on startup. This overrides the preferences value and is primarily intended for testing.
- **safe-plugins**—Runs the plug-in processes inside the sandbox.
- **silent-dump-on-dcheck**—Change the DCHECKS to dump memory and continue instead of crashing. This is valid only in Release mode when --enable-dcheck is specified.
- **single-process**—Runs the renderer and plug-ins in the same process as the browser.

11

- **start-maximized**—Start the browser maximized, regardless of any previous settings. Used as a workaround for not being able to use moveTo and resizeTo on a top-level window.

- **start-renderers-manually**—When this switch is present, the browser throws up a dialog box asking the user to start a renderer process independently rather than launching the renderer itself. (This is useful for debugging.)

- **tab-count-to-load-on-session-restore**—Used to set the value of SessionRestore::num_tabs_to_load. See session_restore for details.

- **test-sandbox**—Runs the security test for the sandbox.

- **testing-channel**—The value of this switch tells the app to listen for and broadcast testing-related messages on IPC channel with the given ID.

- **testshell-startup-dialog**—Causes the test shell process to display a dialog on launch.

- **trusted-plugins**—Excludes these plug-ins from the plug-in sandbox. This is a comma separated list of the plug-in dll's name and ActiveX clsid.

- **Uninstall**—Runs uninstallation steps that were done by Chrome first-run.

- **use-lf-heap**—Use the low fragmentation heap for the CRT.

- **user-data-dir**—Specifies the user data directory, which is where the browser will look for all of its state.

- **wait-for-debugger-children**—Adds WaitForDebugger to every child process. If a value is passed, it is used as a filter to determine if the child process should have the WaitForDebugger flag passed on or not.

Command-line switches are one way to add profile-type capabilities to your Chrome browser. You can also use these switches to perform basic filtering capabilities for Chrome. Either way, it's just a little more functionality that you might not know is available for Chrome.

About...Chrome's Special *about:* Pages

One last thing before we call this chapter complete. Along the path to this particular page in this book, you may have noticed that there were times when an *about:* command was used. For example, in Chapter 5, "Stability on the Net," we looked a little at the *about:crash* command.

It might interest you to know that there are a bunch of other *about:* commands that you can use within Chrome. And some of them can lead you to some pretty interesting information. For example, about:terms takes you to the Google Terms of Service and about:plugins shows information about the plug-ins you have installed in your browser and in other applications on your hard drive.

Just as a refresher, you use the about: command by typing it (followed by the word used for the desired information) into the Omnibar and then pressing **Enter**. When you do, Chrome reloads and provides the requested information. For example, if you type about:stats, a page of useful statistics, like the one shown in Figure 11.17 appears.

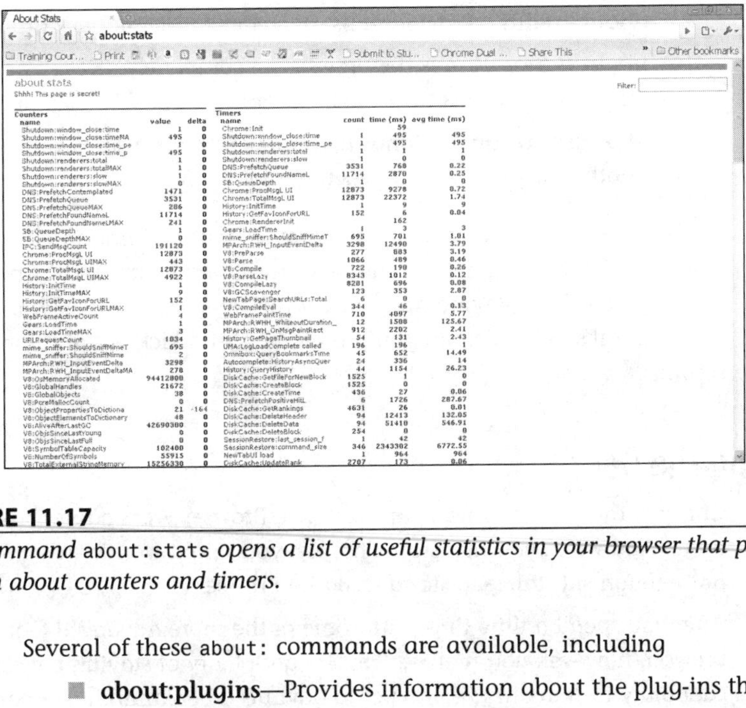

FIGURE 11.17

The command about:stats *opens a list of useful statistics in your browser that provides information about counters and timers.*

Several of these about: commands are available, including

- **about:plugins**—Provides information about the plug-ins that you use with your browser and other applications.

- **about:version**—Provides information about the version of Google Chrome that you're using.

- **about:network**—Provides information about the network to which you're connected.

- **about:stats**—Provides information about statistics that show how resources on your system are being used, including how pages are cached and how Gears behave.
- **about:memory**—Provides information about memory usage within Chrome and other active browsers.
- **about:histograms**—Provides information about histograms.
- **about:dns**—Provides DNS information for the last two hostnames and the last seven pre-fetches.
- **about:cache**—Provides a list of links to the websites in your cache.
- **about:crash**—Forces the current window to crash.
- **about:terms**—Takes you to Google's Terms of Service.
- **about:credits**—Provides a list of credits for available Chrome elements.
- **about:hang**—Hangs the browser up completely. (Developers use it to diagnose problems with the browser.)
- **about:shorthang**—Hangs the browser up for a short while. (This is another one that developers use a lot.)

Go ahead, give it a try. You might be amazed at the information that you learn while you're poking around with the *about:* commands. And one more thing while you're playing around. Try this one: *about:internets*. I won't claim that it's valuable, but you'll probably get a kick out of it for a few seconds.

Closing the Door

Chrome, the newest browser in the whole Browser Wars game, has a lot to live up to. And when you first start Chrome, you might wonder whether it really has enough substance to stand in Battle Browser.

After you spend a little time with some of the more advanced features of the browser, however, you realize, "Yes. It's got plenty of staying power." From the capability to skin out the browser to advanced bookmarking capabilities and the information that you can extract from the browser if you know the right command, Chrome has what it takes.

That's not say you won't experience occasional problems with Chrome. It is designed to be faster, safer, and more efficient than other browsers, but things happen, and once in a while a problem occurs. Not to worry. In Chapter 12,

"Troubleshooting Google Chrome," we address some of the most common problems that you might encounter with Chrome and help you overcome those problems with some detailed answers. So, don't give up just yet. We're almost there, but not quite.

11

CHAPTER

Troubleshooting Google Chrome

Google Chrome is pretty easy to use, but once in a while, you might experience problems with it. Whether it's a problem in the way the browser works or a problem in the way that it installs, most problems are easy enough to address. Of course, there are still those occasional stubborn problems that leave you little choice but to uninstall Chrome and reinstall it.

You should get into the habit of backing up all your addresses, bookmarks, and other settings in Chrome in case you have to uninstall and reinstall the browser due to some strangeness. That backup file could save you hours of trying to re-create the information and settings that you use in Chrome on a daily basis.

Once you've created a backup, remember to update it frequently. Fortunately, not many of the problems that you encounter will result in your having to uninstall and reinstall the browser. The majority of the problems you face should be easily fixed. The remainder of this chapter is dedicated to answering some of the most common questions about difficulties that you might experience while using Chrome.

I installed Chrome, but when I try to type something into the Omnibox, it's wicked slow. What's wrong?

Part of the problem could be that you have too many bookmarks on your Bookmarks bar. Try dragging some of the bookmarks off to the Bookmarks folders and see whether that increases the speed of typing in the Omnibox.

Another problem could be that there's something amiss with the installation of Chrome. Try uninstalling and reinstalling the program to see if that might fix the problems that you're experiencing. (If you need a refresher on how to install Chrome, flip back to Chapter 3, "Getting Started with Google Chrome.")

Chrome crashed, and now I can't get it to stay up without crashing again after a few seconds. Do I need to reinstall it?

You might, but before you do, try this:

Rename your **Default** folder to **Backup**. If you don't remember how to get to the Default folder, navigate to one of these locations on your computer (and remember to replace *<user>* with your username for the computer):

Windows XP: \Documents and Settings*<user>*\Local Settings\Application Data\Google\Chrome\User Data\

Windows Vista: \Users*<user>*\AppData\Local\Google\Chrome\User Data\

If Google Chrome continues to crash after you rename the folder, then move it from the **User Data** directory up one level to the **Chrome** directory. This makes accessing the directly slightly easier, and reduces the number of levels down that the relevant information is located.

Still, it's possible that this solution won't work for you. If that's the case, you'll need to uninstall and reinstall Google Chrome. Fortunately, that's not the worst solution in the world, as it takes about three minutes to download and install Chrome over a broadband connection.

I can't find my bookmarks. I know I created them, but they're not there. What can I do to locate them?

You have a couple of options for finding bookmarks that possibly ended up in the wrong file or folder. First, you can find nine of your most recent links listed in the **Recent Bookmarks** module on right side of the **New Tab** page. It doesn't matter what folder the bookmark was placed in, if it's one of the last nine that you created, you'll be able to click it from this location and be taken to the bookmarked page.

Alternatively, you can also find this list by clicking the **Recently Added** option on the left side of the **Bookmark Manager**. After you've clicked **Recently Added** you'll see a list of the bookmarks that you've created, ordered from the most recent to the oldest. This list includes the Title of the bookmark, the URL of the bookmark, and the Folder the bookmark was created in.

Find the entry that you're looking for, and then you can see what folder the bookmark was created in. If you want to move it to another folder, you'll need to navigate (in the Bookmark Manager) to the folder that the bookmark is currently stored in, then drag it into the folder in the Bookmark Manager where you actually want the link to reside. Once you've dropped the link in a different folder, it's automatically moved without any more input from you.

Chrome has frozen up, and I can't close it. How do I force close the browser?

You need to use the Task Manager to force close a tab or the whole browser. You can access that by selecting **Page Controls, Developer, Task Manager**. Then highlight the item that you want to close (browser or tab) and click the **End Process** button. That closes the tab (or the browser) so that you can start over again. Be aware that any information on tabs or in the browser that you force close is lost.

The text on the web pages I'm viewing looks distorted or strange. What's wrong with Chrome?

It could be that Chrome is attempting to decode the fonts used on the web page using the wrong decoding language. To fix that problem open the **Page** menu and select **Encoding, Auto Detect**. That option allows Chrome to automatically detect the encoding used for the web page. Once enabled, the text on the web pages you're visiting should display properly.

Once you've changed the encoding options for your browser, you'll need to reload the pages that didn't display properly to begin with. If they still aren't displaying correctly, the problem may be in the website, and not in your browser. Unfortunately, if that's the case, you can't control the web page, so there isn't anything that you'll be able to do to improve the display.

I tried to update Chrome's theme, but every time I reopen the browser, all I get is an ugly red color around the edges of the browser window. What did I do wrong?

> You may not have done anything at all wrong. Whether a theme of your choosing works in Chrome depends on which version of Chrome the theme was designed for. It may simply be that you're using a newer (or an older) version of Chrome that's not compatible with the theme that you selected.

Help! I changed the theme on my browser but forgot to back up my default.dll file before I deleted it. Now the theme isn't working properly, and I can't get the original Chrome theme back. What do I do?

> Ouch! You might just have a problem. If you didn't back up the original default.dll file before you deleted it, you might not have any options other than changing to a different theme. Before you give up though, check your **Recycling Bin**. Unless you've emptied it or set it up to be emptied automatically, the original default.dll file might be in the Recycling Bin. If so, you can restore it to the last location, and then replace the offending .dll file with the actual default.dll.

> If all else fails, you will probably have to uninstall the corrupt version of Chrome and reinstall a new one. Don't forget, after you uninstall the old version, restart your computer completely to erase all traces of the previous version of Chrome before you try to install the new version. Otherwise, you could end up with the same problem.

I've downloaded and installed Chrome several times, but it keeps disappearing. I'm using Microsoft Windows Vista. What's the deal?

> Unfortunately, the issue that you're having with Chrome isn't localized to Chrome. It's a larger issue with which Windows Vista is struggling. Something causes files and applications to disappear after installation. An exact cure for this problem has not been found at the time of this writing; however, there seems to be some consensus that this could be a System Mechanic problem. System Mechanic is a suite of software designed to improve the performance of your computer. Turning off System Mechanic might solve the problem. Try turning it off while you're installing the program and then re-enabling System Mechanic once the install is finished.

> If you have a different operating system and you're experiencing the same problem, or even if you're on Vista and don't use System Mechanic and you're

still having the problem, it could be a security application problem. Try disabling all of your system security applications (antivirus applications, firewalls, etc.) during the installation process. Once you've completed the install, make sure you remember to re-enable these products so that your system is protected.

If none of those options work for you, then you may just have to be patient and keep trying to install Chrome periodically. The guys at Google are working on the issue, but as of this writing, they still haven't been able to locate the exact problem.

My Facebook page isn't displaying properly. Is this a Facebook glitch or a Chrome glitch?

The truth is, the glitch that keeps interfering with Facebook is part Facebook issue and part Chrome issue. Developers on both sides are working furiously to get Facebook to consistently render well in Chrome. Until that happens, try it; it might work well for you. And if it doesn't, you might try accessing Facebook from another browser. Just remember to try it again in Chrome frequently because functionalities change in Chrome every single day.

I'm trying to change my home page in Chrome, but it won't update properly. What's going on?

This is a temporary glitch that occurs randomly (but rarely) in Chrome. Keep trying to update your home page URL (maybe over the course of a few days) until the functionality is released and available to you. At this time, there's no rhyme or reason to when or why this happens. But it does seem to clear up all on its own after a short while.

12

I really want to use Chrome as my default browser, but every time I try to set it as the default the option is unavailable. Why can't I make it the default browser?

This is another of those strange glitches that seems to come and go. There are a few options at your disposal, however, that may address it. The first is to keep trying. Eventually, the option may be available to you (that's what worked for me).

If you're not one of those "Wait and let fate sort it out," people, then you might prefer a more proactive approach. If that's the case, there are a couple of things that you can try.

First, you may need to set Chrome up to run in compatibility mode for whatever version if you're using an older version of Microsoft Windows. To do that, right click on the Chrome icon on your desktop and select **Properties**. Then in the Google Chrome Properties dialog box that appears, select the **Compatibility** tab. Once on that tab, select the checkbox next to **Run this program in compatibility mode for:**.

When that option is checked, a drop-down menu becomes available. Select your operating system from that drop-down menu. Your choices are: Windows 95, Windows 98/ME, Windows NT 4.0 (Service Pack 5), or Windows 2000. Unfortunately, there are no other operating systems available at this time.

If you're running Windows Vista and you can't set Chrome as your default from the Chrome Options menu, then you might be able to make it your default from the Vista Default Programs menu. As confusing as that sounds, it's not hard to do.

From the **Start** menu, select **Default Programs** in the menu on the right side (alternatively, you can navigate to this same folder by choosing **Start, Control Panel, Programs, Default Programs**). When the Default Programs dialog box opens, select **Set your default programs.**

In the list on the left side of the dialog box, click **Google Chrome** and then choose **Set this program as default** on the right side of the dialog box. Click **OK** and your settings are saved and you're returned to the initial Default Programs window. You can close this window out, and Chrome should be set as your default browser.

To check if Chrome is indeed the default browser, open Chrome back up, and then select the wrench icon. From the menu that appears, click **Options.** When the Options dialog box opens click the **Basics** tab (if the window doesn't open to that tab automatically). Under Default Browser, the button to click to **Make Google Chrome my default browser** should be grayed out, and there should be a message above it in green that reads "The default browser is currently Google Chrome."

I see all these different version numbers for Chrome. The one I'm using is in the 1s, but I've also seen version numbers for 2, 3, and 4 as well. Which one is the right version number?

To start with, several versions of Chrome are floating around out there. Consumers like you and I are using one version while technogeeks are using another and developers are using yet another version. So, the disparate version numbers that you see could be related to those different versions of Chrome being available.

When in doubt about whether your version of Chrome is properly updated, go to the wrench icon and select **About Google Chrome**. A dialog box appears where the version number for your installation of Chrome is displayed along with a message about whether the version you're using is the most up-to-date. If you need to upgrade, the upgrade link is available here.

I don't like the arrangement of the most visited pages on Chrome's new tab when it opens. How can I change that?

The short answer is you can't. The long answer is that you can restart from the beginning, if you want. The best way to reset the most visited pages is to clear your browser's history. That means selecting that everything except passwords and usernames be cleared from your browsing data.

It's easy enough to do. Just open your browser and select the Tools menu. On the menu that appears, click **Clear browsing data**. This opens a dialog box that allows you to select the items that you would like to have cleared. Make sure the checkboxes next to **Clear browsing history** and **Empty the cache** are selected and then select **Everything** from the **Clear data from this period** drop-down menu. Next click **Clear Browsing Data.** It might take a little while for all of the data to be cleared from your browser, but once it is, the browser will refresh and your Most visited area will be blank. Now you can start all over again, creating the pages that you use most often.

The best way to reset your Most visited pages is to just visit the top nine sites that you want displayed on that page. You may even want to visit those sites several times just to be sure they don't get bumped when you're doing some random surfing. And remember, those pages are displayed in the order of most visited to least visited, so there is no guarantee that the specific order you set up those pages in will remain the same over time.

Sometimes when I close out of Google Chrome, I get a Trojan warning from my antivirus software that includes the chrome.exe file. Help! Do I have a Trojan and what do I do?

If the notification that you're getting is coming from your antivirus software, and the notification says that the Trojan has been blocked, then you're probably safe. If the notification tells you that you need to perform additional actions to remove or destroy the Trojan, follow the prompts in the notification.

Beyond the issue of the antivirus application, there's also the worrisome fact that there's a Trojan attacking your installation of Chrome. It's likely that you've picked this Trojan up on some website that you've visited. I experienced

12

the same issues with my installation of Chrome and traced the Trojan back to a website on which I play a game (www.bubbleshooter.net). The fact that you're getting the notification probably means that the Trojan has been blocked, quarantined, or removed. So, the first thing that you'll need to do is alter your behavior. If you can isolate the site where you picked up the nasty little bugger, stay away from it.

Then, uninstall your current instance of Chrome and restart your computer. After you restart the computer, you can download and install a new installation of Chrome. But do it directly from the Chrome website (www.google.com/chrome), rather than using files that might exist on your computer. If you have installation files on your computer from a previous installation, it's wise to delete those files and start completely from scratch, just in case there's an issue with the previously installed version of the software.

Suddenly, Chrome has started locking up. When I'm surfing a web page, it will start to load and then just hang. The page won't change, I won't get an error message, and sometimes I have to force close the browser. What's up?

One thing that you need to keep in mind while you're using Chrome is that it's a virtual infant. Strange and unexplained things are going to happen, and this is one of them. For whatever reason, Chrome occasionally hangs up. It could be that something in the rendering process gets stuck, or there could be one of a hundred other issues at play. No matter what's causing it, though, it's frustrating if you're trying to get to a website. So how do you get around the issue?

Try copying the URL from the Omnibox for the page that's hanging up, and then pasting that address into the Omnibox of a new tab. The page should then load smoothly, and you can close the previous tab that wasn't working properly. It's a bit frustrating, but the work around helps you to continue along your surfing journey without getting lost. The one thing that you should remember, though, is that you'll never be able to use the Back button to go further back than the page you got hung up on.

I use WordPress to create my blog, but when I access WordPress in Chrome, the only controls that are available to me are the publishing controls. I can't change times, add categories, or change post authors. What's going on?

This is a glitch in Chrome. At the time this book was written, this glitch had been reported, but had not been repaired. There also does not seem to be a workaround for this problem. It turns out you'll have to use a different browser to manage your WordPress blog, at least for the time being.

Appendices

Google Chrome Shortcuts

Keyboard shortcuts are key combinations that help you reduce the amount of mouse use you need to perform a specific action. The theory is that it takes far less time and energy to press a combination of keys on the keyboard than it does to reach over, align the mouse, and then click the button to create the action you want.

The problem comes in when you don't know the keyboard shortcuts. With Google Chrome, some of the keyboard shortcuts that you've become familiar with in other browsers have the same functions. There are some new combinations, though. What follows is a specific list of the available keyboard shortcuts for Chrome. Even if you think you know them all, you might want to scan the list. You could find something that you didn't know exists.

Navigation Shortcuts

The shortcuts in the following table are designed to help you navigate through windows, tabs, and web pages. You may already know many of them, but a few are specific to Chrome.

Keyboard Shortcut	Function
Ctrl+N	Open a new window.
Ctrl+T	Open a new tab.
Ctrl+Shift+N	Open a new window in Incognito mode.
Ctrl+O then select file	Open a file from your computer in Google Chrome.
Crtl+click a link	Open link in a new background tab while remaining on the current tab.
Ctrl+Shift+click a link	Open link in a new tab and switch to the newly opened tab.
Shift+click a link	Open link in a new window.
Alt+F4	Close current window.
Ctrl+Shift+T	Reopen the last tab you closed. Google Chrome remembers the last 10 tabs you closed.
Drag link to tab	Open link in specified tab.
Drag link to space between tabs	Open link in a new tab in the specified position on the tab strip.
Ctrl+1 through Ctrl+8	Switch to the tab at the specified position number. The number you press represents the position of the tab on the tab strip.
Ctrl+9	Switch to the last tab.
Ctrl+Tab or Ctrl+PgDown	Switch to the next tab.
Ctrl+Shift+Tab or Ctrl+PgUp	Switch to the previous tab.
Ctrl+W or Ctrl+F4	Close current tab or pop-up.
Alt+Home	Open your home page.
Backspace or press Alt+left arrow	Go to the previous page in your browsing history for the tab.
Shift+Backspace or press Alt+right arrow	Go to the next page in your browsing history for the tab.
Ctrl+K or Ctrl+E	Place a question mark in the address bar. Type a search term after the question mark to perform a search using your default search engine.
Place your cursor in the address bar then press Ctrl+left arrow	Jump to the previous word in the address bar.
Place your cursor in the address bar then press Ctrl+right arrow	Jump to the next word in the address bar.

A

Keyboard Shortcut	Function
Place your cursor in the address bar then press Ctrl+Backspace	Delete the previous word in the address bar.
Space bar	Scroll down the web page.
Home	Go to the top of the page.
End	Go to the bottom of the page.

Address Bar Shortcuts

The address bar, also called the Omnibox, has much more functionality than simply taking you to a web address. The following shortcuts help you to access as much of that functionality as possible.

Keyboard Shortcut	Function
Type a search term	Perform a search using your default search engine.
Type the part of the web address that's between *www.* and *.com* then press Ctrl+Enter	Add www. and .com to your input in the address bar and open the web address.
Type a search engine keyword or URL, press Tab, then type a search term	Perform a search using the search engine associated with the keyword or the URL. Google Chrome prompts you to press Tab if it recognizes the search engine you're trying to use.
F6 or Ctrl+L or Alt+D	Highlight content in the web address area.
Type a web address then press Alt+Enter	Open your web address in a new tab.

Chrome Feature Shortcuts

The shortcuts in the following table allow you to access certain Chrome features quickly and without having to navigate through a bunch of menus to find what you need. Some of these shortcuts are real time-savers, so be sure you read through them to find the ones you might not know about.

Keyboard Shortcut	Function
Ctrl+B	Toggle bookmarks bar on and off.
Ctrl+Shift+B	Open the Bookmark manager.
Ctrl+H	View the History page.
Ctrl+J	View the Downloads page.
Shift+Escape	View the Task manager.
Shift+Alt+T	Set focus on the toolbar. Use right and left arrows on the keyboard to navigate to different buttons on the toolbar.

A

Web Page Shortcuts

Navigating web pages without a mouse might be a foreign concept to you. And in truth, you probably can't do everything with the keyboard that you might want to do on a web page, but you can do plenty of things. These keyboard shortcuts help you navigate through the web pages that you choose to surf.

Keyboard Shortcut	Function
Ctrl+P	Print your current page
Ctrl+S	Save your current page
F5	Reload current page
Esc	Stop page loading
Ctrl+F5 or Shift+F5	Reload current page, ignoring cached content
Press Alt + click a link	Download link
Ctrl+F	Open find-in-page box
Ctrl+G or F3	Find next match for your input in the find-in-page box
Ctrl+Shift+G or Shift+F3	Find previous match for your input in the find-in-page box
Ctrl+U	View source
Drag link to bookmarks bar	Bookmark the link
Ctrl+D	Bookmark your current web page
Ctrl++	Make text larger
Ctrl+-	Make text smaller
Ctrl+0	Return to normal text size

Text Shortcuts

The last few shortcuts in this appendix are all related to text content. In most cases, you need to highlight text or place your cursor where you want text to appear before you perform an action. These are all pretty basic, and you probably use some of them with other programs, but there might be one or two here that you haven't seen.

A

Keyboard Shortcut	Function
Ctrl+C	Copy content to the Clipboard
Ctrl+V or Shift+Insert	Paste current content from the Clipboard
Ctrl+Shift+V	Paste current content from the Clipboard without formatting
Ctrl+X or Shift+Delete	Delete the content and copy it to the Clipboard

A

Chrome for the Non-Windows User

If you're familiar with Linux or Macintosh operating systems, you may have wondered if there is a Google Chrome for those platforms. While the official versions of Chrome for Linux and Chrome for Mac haven't been released yet, there is a way to run Chrome on your Linux or Mac machine.

CrossOver Chromium

Up until now, we've talked about the official versions of Google Chrome and Chromium. These applications only work on computers running Microsoft Windows. Google tells us that versions of Chrome for *Linux* and *Mac OS X* are on the way. It's possible they might even be released by the time you're reading these words; however, at the time of this writing, Google has not given a target date.

Linux is an operating system was originally developed by Linus Torvalds in 1991. Linux is, and always has been, an open source operating system. As a result, there are many different "brands" or distributions of Linux. Red Hat, Ubuntu, and Debian are some names you may be familiar with. Each distribution is an improvement or change on an earlier distribution.

Mac OS X is the operating system used by Apple's Macintosh computers. Mac OS X has been the standard operating system for Macintosh computers since 2002, although, it has been updated frequently since then. Mac OS X is proprietary software and is owned entirely by Apple, Inc.

Granted, the Linux and Mac markets are smaller than the Windows market, but Linux users tend to be active in the open source programming scene. The long wait for an official Google Chrome release has annoyed several outspoken open source gurus. However, in true open source fashion the Linux and Mac communities didn't wait for Google.

A software development company, called *Codeweavers*, stepped in. They created and released CrossOver Chromium for both Mac and Linux users.

Codeweavers defines itself as a company striving to transform Mac OS X and Linux into Windows-compatible operating systems, helping customers leverage Windows technology on non-Windows operating systems, and promoting growth of Free Software by supporting and extending the Wine Project.

They created and distribute the CrossOver line of products.

CrossOver Linux gives those running most of the popular Linux distributions the ability to run Windows based applications like Microsoft Office, Dreamweaver MX, Microsoft Project, and many more.

CrossOver Mac gives Mac OS X users the same flexibility to run applications and open files intended for Microsoft Windows operating systems, without purchasing a Windows license.

CrossOver Games lets both Linux and Mac OS X users run gaming applications intended for Microsoft Windows.

You can find Codeweavers at http://www.codeweavers.com/.

CrossOver Chromium runs Chromium through *Wine*, making the necessary tweaks to Chromium for you. So you get a working version of Chromium out of the box. After evaluating CrossOver Chromium on Ubuntu 8.10 Intrepid Ibex, I can say that it does work well. CrossOver Chromium is a bit slower than Chrome or Chromium run on Windows, and the graphics don't seem to be as sharp, but both are to be expected when you run any program through Wine. The process of having an intermediary program between the application you're running and the operating system can cause slower performance and slightly fuzzy text.

geek speak

Wine is a small application that serves as a translator between the Linux or Mac operating system and an application designed to work with the Microsoft Windows protocol. When you run a Windows-based program in Wine, the Windows program talks directly to Wine, and then Wine translates and relays the requests to the Linux or Mac components.

Wine stands for Wine Is Not an Emulator. You will find Wine for Linux, and BSD at http://www.winehq.org/. Although there is no official Wine release for Mac OS X, those running that operating system can use Wine. Instructions are provided on the Wine website here: http://wiki.winehq.org/MacOSX/Installing. Mac users can find additional step-by-step directions for installing Wine on David Baumgold's website, here: http://davidbaumgold.com/tutorials/wine-mac/.

Installing CrossOver Chromium for both Linux and Mac is painless. No tweaking is needed; just install and go. Installation for Linux and Mac is covered in detail in the following sections.

Linux

CrossOver Chromium works with most Linux distributions. The test computer for instructions runs Ubuntu 8.10 with Firefox 3.0.8. Your download procedure may be different, depending on the flavor of Linux you use and your web browser.

Visit http://www.codeweavers.com/services/ports/chromium/ and download the application version for your operating system. As with all open source

B

software, be sure to read through the FAQs. If you are installing CrossOver Chromium right away, make sure to select **Open with** (and have your preferred package manager selected). If you are downloading to install later, select **Save File**. Click **OK**. Figure B.1 shows the download window.

> You have chosen to open
>
> ☐ **cxchromium_0.9.0-1_i386.deb**
>
>   which is a: Software package
>   from: http://media.codeweavers.com
>
> **What should Firefox do with this file?**
>
>   ◉ O_pen with | GDebi Package Installer (default) | ⌄ |
>
>   ○ _Save File
>
>   ☐ Do this _automatically for files like this from now on.
>
>   ❌ Cancel   ⬅ OK

FIGURE B.1

If applicable, select your package manager.

If you'd rather use the *command terminal* to download, the command is

```
wget http://media.codeweavers.com/pub/crossover/chromium/
cxchromium_0.9.0-1_i386.deb
```

Enter this in the terminal on one line.

geek speak The command terminal is where users enter code to control the computer, instead of using the mouse, as in Microsoft Windows. To access the command terminal in Ubuntu select **Applications, Accessories, Terminal**.

Once you've downloaded the install package and opened it (either automatically or manually), a window appears, similar to Figure B.2. It asks whether you want to install the program. Select **Install**. If you are reinstalling the CrossOver Chromium, select **Reinstall Package**, as shown in the figure. You are prompted to enter your system password. After you do so, Crossover Chromium installs. That's all there is to it. Wasn't that easy?

If you're using the command terminal, the install command is

```
sudo dpkg -i cxchromium_0.9.0-1_i386.deb
```

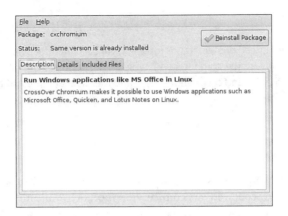

FIGURE B.2

The appearance of this screen depends on your Linux distro and your package manager.

You are prompted for your password. Remember, many Linux distros do not show your password as you type.

To run CrossOver Chromium from your *GUI*, select **Applications, CrossOver Chromium, Chromium** from the menu bar, as illustrated in Figure B.3.

FIGURE B.3

Launching Chromium from the menu bar. Your menu bar will look different depending on your Linux distribution.

geek speak

GUI, pronounced *goo-ee*, stands for *Graphical User Interface*. This is the method of interfacing with the computer with which most people are familiar. You use your mouse to point and click various icons and menus that represent the applications you want to use.

Mac OS X

If you're using Mac OS X, you can download CrossOver Chromium from http://www.codeweavers.com/services/ports/chromium/.

Click on the link below the heading Apple Mac OS X. As shown in Figure B.4, the download manager opens. Select to **Open with** your package manager to install right away, or **Save File** to install later. Click **OK**.

```
 ○ ○ ○          Opening cxchromium-0.9.0.dmg

 You have chosen to open
  ▣ cxchromium-0.9.0.dmg
    which is a: DMG file
    from: http://media.codeweavers.com

 What should Firefox do with this file?

  ⦿ Open with    DiskImageMounter.app (default)   ⬍
  ○ Save File
  ☐ Do this automatically for files like this from now on.

                        ( Cancel )   ( OK )
```

FIGURE B.4

Download the DMG file with your download manager. If you're not using Firefox, this window may appear differently.

After CrossOver Chromium has downloaded, you see a screen similar to Figure B.5. Left-click on the **CrossOver Chromium icon** and drag it to the Applications icon. As you can see in Figure B.6, CrossOver Chromium is now in your Applications folder.

B

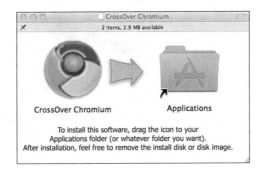

FIGURE B.5

Installing CrossOver Chromium is as easy as drag and drop.

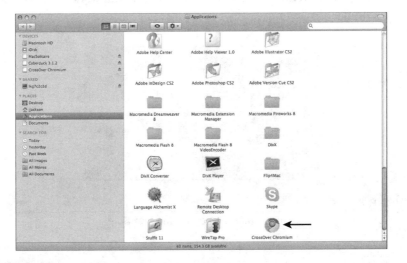

FIGURE B.6

CrossOver Chromium can now be seen in your Applications folder.

To run CrossOver Chromium for the first time, double-click the **CrossOver Chromium icon** in the Applications folder. A window opens asking whether you're sure you want to run this program that has been downloaded from the Internet. Click **Open**. Figure B.7 shows how this window may look.

B

FIGURE B.7

This warning dialog helps protect your computer from programs downloaded without your knowledge.

When CrossOver Chromium initializes and opens you see a dialog box similar to Figure B.8. After the initialization sequence, CrossOver Chromium opens to the Most Visited page, as shown in Figure B.9. Enter the URL you want to visit and press **Enter**. From here, CrossOver Chromium works just like Google Chrome in Windows.

FIGURE B.8

CrossOver Chromium is getting ready to open for the first time.

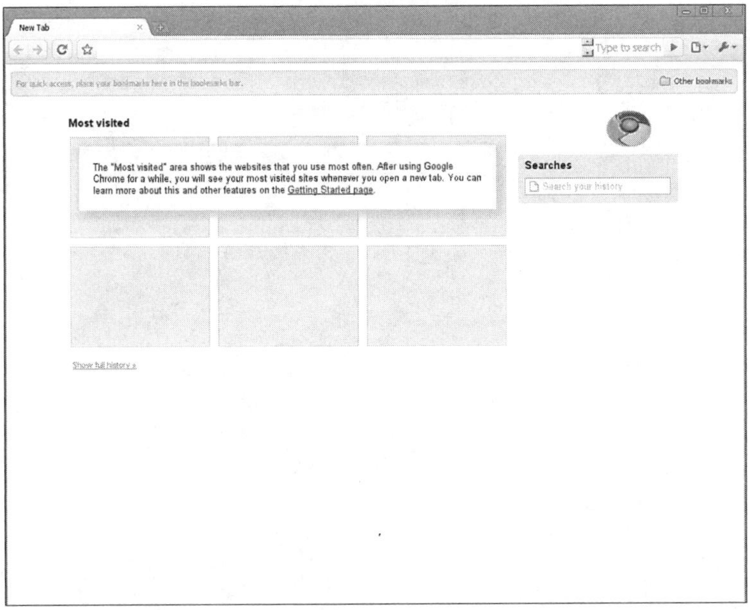

FIGURE B.9
The landing page looks just like the official version of Google Chrome.

As you can see, CrossOver Chromium gives Linux and Mac OS X users the ability to try out Chromium without using the Microsoft Windows operating system. You probably shouldn't use CrossOver Chromium for your heavy browsing needs, since running through Wine deteriorates the speed and clarity of graphics. But, if you just want to play around with Chromium, or you aren't a power user, CrossOver Chromium does the job nicely.

B

Glossary

Acid tests   A series of tests designed to challenge the way a given web browser translates and renders HTML and XML. Acid tests also test the JavaScript capabilities of the browser. You can find out exactly what is involved in Acid testing, and even run Acid tests on your web browsers at the Web Standards Project Acid Tests website: http://www.acidtests.org/.

add-ins   Bits of applications, or mini-applications, that offer additional functionality that operate with an application. Add-ins are usually used to reference browsers and other applications, such as Microsoft Word.

android   A mobile device operating system developed by Google and the Open Handset Alliance.

Application Programming Interface   A set of commands that allow a developer to access functions in one program from within another program. Think of it as a set of hooks that allow the programmer to join the functions of two programs.

ARM instruction set   Refers to the machine language dialect of the processors in most mobile devices.

back-end functions   Small programs embedded or plugged into larger applications. These smaller programs provide added capabilities.

benchmarking   A frequently used term in computer jargon for submitting an application (Chrome in this case) for rigorous performance testing using industry standard tests to measure performance. These results allow technologists and consumers to compare hardware and software objectively.

bookmarklets   Mini-applications that you can run from your bookmarks. These work like gadgets or widgets; they're small applications with a bit of functionality used by the whole program they represent.

cache   A collection of copies of websites that you've visited. These copies are stored in a location on your hard drive so that they can be used to help pages load faster if you return to the same website.

Cascading Style Sheets   See *style sheet*.

command-line switches   Parameters that can be added to the command line when starting Chrome that make it behave slightly differently than if the command-line switches were not there. These switches enable or disable functionality such as Java, images, and metrics reporting.

cookie   A bit of information that's added to your browser cache when you visit a website. This information is used to both track your movements while you're on the website that gave you the cookie and help track your preferences on the site. As a general rule, cookies aren't harmful, though there is some concern that cookies could violate your privacy by allowing companies to track your movements beyond their websites.

developer browser   A browser designed for use by developers. Often, that means a separate toolbar that attaches to your browser that allows you to validate code and view web pages as if you were in a development environment.

DNS (Domain Name System)   A translator of sorts that is in charge of assigning domain names to IP addresses, which are the actual web addresses of websites. When a website is called from a web browser, the DNS must convert what you enter into the browser's address bar (www.website.com) into an address that the server can understand (123.456.7.8) before the website can be displayed.

DNS pre-fetching   When an IP address is fetched before it's called for. Think of it this way. If you have Rover go fetch the paper at a certain time every day, eventually, he might begin to understand that you're going to want that paper. So, rather than waiting for you to tell him to go get it, he picks it up on his own and drops it on the porch steps (instead of leaving it out by the street). Then, when you want the paper, he only has to go to the porch to retrieve it, which makes the whole process faster. It's the same concept with DNS pre-fetching.

extensions   Bits of functionality that extend the usability of the browser. For example, a Firefox extension called FireFTP is an FTP application that works within your browser to allow you to access and interact with FTP sites.

fragmentation   When memory is assigned and unassigned repeatedly in an application, it causes fragmentation. When the memory is unassigned, it leaves little "potholes" in its place, which adversely affects performance. See also: *Fragmented disk.*

fragmented disk   A condition that happens when files are moved around your hard drive. Think of the hard drive as blocks of information. The larger the block, the more you can do with it. Over time, the single large block that is your hard drive is divided into tons of small ones, and as programs and data are moved around, large areas are blocked off, or freed up. When the free spaces are all interrupted by the blocked spaces, they become less usable. The resulting disk fragmentation can make large areas of your hard drive harder to access, even though there's nothing on them. Realigning all the blocks of data helps to create larger areas of free space that are easier (and faster) to access.

function   A reusable block of code that tells the computer how to perform a specific task. Functions are called, or used, when the user clicks a link, opens a file, or otherwise gives a command for the computer to do something.

gadgets   They're bits of applications, or mini-applications, that offer additional functionality that operates with an application. You see gadgets used more often in reference to sidebar applications and add-ins.

Greasemonkey   An extension originally developed for Mozilla Firefox that lets the user run small lines of JavaScript to add features to, or change the appearance of a website.

inline caching   A method by which copies of web page code are held at the ready in case you need to use them. For inline caching, those copies are held on the same memory as other programs on your computer, rather than deeper in the system. This allows the pages that are cached to be accessed much quicker than if they were to be pulled from another location.

installer   Allows you to download a single executable file that "weighs" a fraction of the entire application size so that you can download the file at a more convenient time. Many installers even keep track of where a download starts so that you may stop a download and resume it at a later time—for example, when there is less Internet traffic—without data loss. Using an installer can also prevent third parties from redistributing an entire software application, forcing the user to still download from the software editor's desired location. The installer is also useful because it's often usable with updates (instead of having to download a new installer), and it's also useful when you change computers, as you're not required to install any additional software.

isolated tabs   Separate processes within a web browser. So, when you open a website in one tab and then open a second website in another tab, the two are entirely separate instances of the web browser wrapped in a single interface. The processes in one tab won't affect the processes in the second tab, so if you experience difficulties—such as a crash—with one of the tabs, the other can continue in its current state without any information on the unaffected tab being lost.

JavaScript engine   An interpreter for your computer. It interprets JavaScript source code into actions. In other words, it decodes a script (that is seemingly in a foreign language) and executes the actions coded into that script.

Java Virtual Machine (JVM)   A set of programs that run Java programs in a virtual environment. This frees resources for other applications, which prevents your system from slowing down when Java is being executed.

KHTML   An HTML rendering engine developed by the same people who came up with the K desktop environment for Unix-like systems. The first version of KHTML was released in late 1998.

KJS   Developed in 2000 as the JavaScript interpreter for KDE's Konqueror web browser.

Linux distros   (Also called distributions) Open source operating systems based on the Linux kernel. Many distros are available to Linux users, and each provides a unique user experience. Red Hat, Debian, and Ubuntu are examples of popular Linux distros. They are the open source equivalent to Windows XP, Windows Vista, Mac OS, and others.

malware   A more generic term used for software designed to gain access to your computer (without your knowledge) and do harm. This can be the classic computer virus, a Trojan horse, spyware, and so on. Whatever form malware takes, it is never good.

markup   A system of noting how text should be displayed onscreen. Typically referred to as *markup languages*, these systems are not real computer languages, since they lack the required components to be considered a language. (By definition, a real programming language must contain tests, branches, and loops.) Some common examples of markup are HTML (HyperText Markup Language) and XML (eXtensible Markup Language).

markup languages   See *Markup*.

memory leak   This has everything to do with how efficiently your system runs, and nothing to do with losing data. Every program borrows memory from the computer to run. When you close that program, it's supposed to give the borrowed memory back. If it doesn't, that's called a memory leak. Typically, the missing memory stays unavailable until you reboot your system.

MIME   An overview term for the various ways data is put together in cyberspace. Some familiar MIME types include application/x-javascript, application/pdf, image/jpg, application/zip, and audio/mpeg.

Open Handset Alliance   A group of mobile technology companies that have come together to work on creating an "open" mobile web. Currently, mobility is ruled by proprietary technologies. You're either with one company or you're with another. The goal of the Open Handset Alliance is to create mobility without borders or walls where mobile devices and mobile applications all work together to achieve a single goal—providing users with the service and applications that they want and need.

out-of-the-box   A term that means you can use the software without any customization at all; you simply download it, install it, and then start using it. Of course, customization might still be possible—tweaking it to your preferences—but it's not required to accomplish the core function of software. In other words, you can use it straight out of the box.

peer-to-peer   Software that allows you to share files stored on your computer with anonymous users all over the world through software called *torrents*. Through websites that act as online directories or catalogs, you can download a torrent that connects to other computers on the network that make any file available for download through the peer-to-peer client software. Since this process is largely anonymous, there's no way of knowing whether the files available from others are corrupt in any way (virus, Trojan, spyware).

phishing   An online scamming technique whereby an ill-intended person sends a bogus email pretending to be from a large or famous website in the hopes of getting you to reveal personal information. For example, an email may claim to be from the World's Largest Bank and that you need to confirm your personal details by clicking the link in the email. The link is often a different or a spoofed web address that snares you in and gets your information once you go for the bait.

Portable Network Graphic (PNG)   A file format for graphics. Portable Network Graphics are commonly used in artwork for the Web.

Remember The Milk   A web application that allows you to create and store your to-do lists online. You'll find it at www.rememberthemilk.com.

RLZ parameter   Made of encoded information about your version of Google Chrome. It includes information like from where you downloaded Chrome, when you installed it, and when you first used specific Chrome features. This information is sent to Google whenever you use Chrome's built-in search bar to perform a search. Google assures users this information is completely anonymous and is only used to evaluate whether specific groups of people are using Chrome.

sandbox   A controlled environment that developers use to run untested code. The idea of the sandbox is to allow processes and applications to be isolated so they cannot alter other processes and applications until they've been tested.

sandboxing   A programming term that means to completely separate a program from the rest of the system. The sandboxed program has its own memory and can't talk to any other program on the computer, much like a child playing alone in her own sandbox.

Secure Sockets Layer (SSL)   A security protocol that encrypts data that's transmitted over the Internet. That includes data transmitted through email as well as data that you enter into forms online.

source code   The instructions that tell the computer what to do. It's written in programming languages such as C++ or Visual Basic and translated into something the computer can understand using a separate program, called a compiler. It is the source code that falls under the various software license types.

SSL 2.0   A security protocol supported by Chrome. The most recent SSL version is 3.0, which should give you an indication of how old it really is. There are a number of compelling reasons not to enable this feature, notably with respect to security itself! SSL 2.0 suffers from several well-known security issues, such as vulnerability to attacks, and also has a weakened MAC structure. As noted, it's better to leave this alone unless you are certain it is supported.

SSL Security   A type of encryption that uses secure certificates for authenticating both the person sending the information and the person receiving it. SSL uses an encryption method that includes both public and private keys. Public keys are the method by which the data is encrypted, and private keys are the method by which it is decoded. Public keys are more widely available, and private keys are only available to the person who is intended to access the protected data.

style sheet   Better known as a Cascading Style Sheet (CSS). A text file that defines the names of the styles used in a website. These styles are then assigned a set of characteristics, or properties, that define the particular style. This consists of the font or font family used, font size, font color, indentations, and so on. When a website is published online, it uses this CSS file (for example, default.css) to define how the page styles appear in the web browser.

user interface   The part of the application that users see and interact with. In terms of our browser comparison, Chrome has few buttons and tools integrated into the part of the browser that you see. On the other hand, Internet Explorer has tons of buttons and tools built right into the top of the browser. For some this is handy; for others, it's clutter.

V8 JavaScript Engine   The Java Virtual Machine on steroids. It not only runs Java apps in a virtual environment, but it also cleans up after itself to keep your resources from being bogged down by bits and pieces of applications that are no longer in use. In other words, it helps your web-based applications and pages run faster.

W3C **(World Wide Web Consortium)**   This organization is made up of member organizations from around the world. Members work together to establish and maintain programming standards for the Internet. To learn more about the W3C, what they do, or how to become a member, check out the official website, http://www.w3.org/.

W3C standards   Define the industry best practices for developing web pages. These standards provide developers with guidelines for everything from page accessibility for the disabled, to using XHTML on web pages. W3C standards are not required; however, most developers comply with the guidelines.

widgets   Bits of applications, or mini-applications, that offer additional functionality that operates with an application. You see widgets used more often in reference to sidebar applications and add-ins.

Windows Mobile   The operating system for mobile devices put out by Microsoft.

X86 instruction set   Refers to the dialect of machine language the computer processor understands. X86 processors run the majority of workstations and laptops in the world.

Index

X–Z

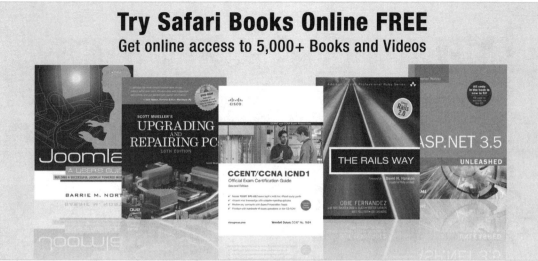

Security · Privacy · Open Source · Web Kit · Chromium · Chrome
Navigation · Customization · Tabbed Browsing · Omnibox · Secu

Jerri Ledford

FREE Online Edition

Your purchase of **Web Geek's Guide to Google™ Chrome** includes access to a free online edition for 45 days through the Safari Books Online subscription service. Nearly every Que book is available online through Safari Books Online, along with more than 5,000 other technical books and videos from publishers such as Addison-Wesley Professional, Cisco Press, Exam Cram, IBM Press, O'Reilly, and Prentice Hall.

SAFARI BOOKS ONLINE allows you to search for a specific answer, cut and paste code, download chapters, and stay current with emerging technologies.

Activate your FREE Online Edition at
www.informit.com/safarifree

> **STEP 1:** Enter the coupon code: TEUDHBI.

> **STEP 2:** New Safari users, complete the brief registration form.
> Safari subscribers, just log in.

If you have difficulty registering on Safari or accessing the online edition, please e-mail customer-service@safaribooksonline.com

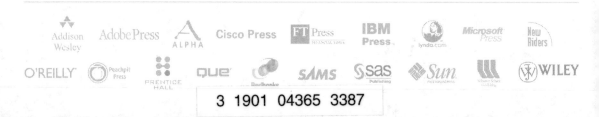